Nine Days In November

Lee Pound

Nine Days in November

Solutions Press
ISBN: 978-0-9846872-7-5
First Edition: September 2025

This is a work of non-fiction. All events described in and after 1993 involved or were witnessed by the author. Events prior to 1993 are based on documents created by Sheri Long. The opinions expressed in this book are those of the author alone.

Dedication

To Sheri Long, who changed my life forever.

To my parents, Ray and Jessie Pound, who welcomed Sheri into the family as if she were their daughter.

To Sherree Jolly and Alice (a pseudonym for a long-time friend of Sheri who requested her name not be used), who helped guide Sheri to her final peace.

Acknowledgements

To Pam Boswell, Sheri's step-sister and life-long friend, for her unwavering support during Sheri's illness, including numerous trips from Santa Barbara to be by Sheri's side every step of the way.

To Yvette LaVigne, her long-time friend and "sisty," and Gale Ekiss, her friend since elementary school in Yuma, for their support and counsel during the roughest days of the last three years.

To Sherree Jolly and Alice and the Saddleback Hospice team for their 24-hour presence during Sheri's last nine days and to Alice for leading all of us on Sheri's final journey to peace and eternity.

To Denise Lamonte, Denise and Michael Moon, Rev. Jim Turrell, Michelle Bogarin, Susan Leone, Dave and Jeannie Sullenger, Jean and Bill Wright, Diane Wood, Bob and Diane Estrada, and Joy Tash for their presence and assistance during Sheri's difficult last month.

To the physicians and nurses at Saddleback Hospital and UCI Medical Center, including Dr. David Imagawa, Dr. Edward Wagner, Dr. Lynn Granlund and Dr. Benjamin Weinberg for their careful and professional service when needed during the two years of her illness.

To my best friend Arvee Robinson and her late husband Michael Jakubowski for their unswerving support for both Sheri and me as we navigated this crisis.

To Clinton Swaine and the Frontier Trainings family for their patient caring and emotional support for Sheri in her time of need. She loves all of you.

To the many colleagues and friends of both Sheri and I for the support, cards, letters, and phone calls we received during Sheri's illness. We could not have gotten through it without you.

Preface

The story in this book changed my life and I hope it will change yours as well.

The story lasted nine days, 2 years, 24 years, and 67 years yet it seems as if it happened in an instant.

If you are not religious, it will give you hope. If you are religious, it will give you perspective.

I wrote it not because it is the story of my wife but because it is the story of all of us.

Like most people, I have been on a spiritual journey of discovery all my life. I grew up with a structured religion that gave certainty at the expense of believability. As I entered my adult life, I had to admit that it gave me no comfort so I abandoned it.

After many years of searching (on and off, not full time), my first wife, who is not part of this book, introduced me to the teachings of Ernest Holmes, which made far more sense to me.

As the years passed, opportunities opened and closed. One seemingly random event led to another seemingly random event, which, when added together and placed in sequence, led to the story I am about to relate.

When I met Sheri, she shared my spiritual philosophy, part of the reason we fell in love in the Spring of 1993.

Yes, this book is about Sheri's life. It is also about my journey with her through marriage, illness, and finally her passing from this earth.

Her story on earth is remarkable but the story of her passing from this earth, her last nine days, is powerful beyond anything I have ever experienced. It is that nine days, and the years that led to it, that I share with you now. It changed my perspective on what life is about, how we must live it to be a light in this world instead of contributing to the darkness we see descending on this world as we grow older.

I now see the light that all of us shine into the darkness. We are all spirits of light, we all have a message to share, a contribution to make, a dark life to illumine. Sheri illuminated more than her share of lives. I wrote this book to inspire you to do the same with your life.

Join me now for a spiritual journey that will leave you first doubting, then marveling, then changing your life forever as it did mine.

Contents

Introduction

Death! So final yet … is it? It arrives with stealth, often in the middle of promises yearning to grow, and cuts off life on the threshold of success. At times, it waits in quiet repose, unconsidered as a possibility, until it strikes with sudden ferocity. At other times, it sneaks into the room when we least expect it, makes its presence known, then waits with a smug smirk while its target squirms and protests, at times for years.

Death took both my parents with sudden ferocity, so fast we had no time to say goodbye.

Death took my wife Sheri Long with a slow crescendo that will change the way you look at life forever. At times it rose, at times faded, then gave hope and took it away, over two long years.

Her last nine days began in slow, painful frustration. Then in a twist none of us expected, Sheri led us on a once-in-a-lifetime spiritual journey to the edge of the awesome reality that awaits us all as we pass from this life.

This is her story.

There is an all-powerful, all-knowing, creative Divine Intelligence that's as inconceivably enormous as the ocean which encompasses EVERYTHING. I'm part of this Divine Intelligence like a drop of H_2O is part of the ocean. We are one. There is NO separating us. There is no power in fear. That's just silly imagination. The TRUTH is that I'm ALWAYS connected to my Source, who knows only perfect health and optimum outcomes for my well-being. I know all my cells are always working together in HARMONY for my perfect health. I'm so grateful for this ever-present ongoing activity. I let go of controlling the outcome cuz I know it's in Divine "Hands." So 'tis.

Sheri Long
August 3, 2015
Wee hours of Monday

Part I

2015
Sunday,
The First Day in November

The Universe is infinite love. I know I'm love individualized. I want you to know that you are pure love, you are loved and you are loving. Love shines brightly through you and gently envelopes all around you. This is a done deal. You've got all the love you need. It's already flowing and growing easily and effortlessly. I let go of any attachments or expectations of the outcome.

Sheri Long
February 7, 2007

ONE

The Beginning of the End, Part 1, Sunday, November 1, 2015

As I write this, I sit on a bench on a cliff above Laguna Beach Main Beach, one of Sheri's favorite places. A few trees shade me on the right. She and I often came here to relax and unwind. It is a beautiful day, warm, not hot. Catalina peeks through the haze in the distance and the horizon is as sharp as a needle.

It is November 12, three days since Sheri left us. She passed as she lived, on her own terms and in her own time. She often showed up late to momentous events. True to form, she passed when she felt ready and not a moment sooner.

As I sit here, I suspect she hovers a few feet away, in the trees, inches beyond human notice, to inspire me to tell this story with the power it deserves and the authority it requires.

A little black bird lands and ambles along a short rock wall, six inches high, until it stands in front of me, two feet away. It chirps as it walks. It looks up at me, unafraid, emits a final loud chirp, and flies away.

Sheri started her flight into eternity Sunday morning, November 1. As I look back over the last two weeks, I find it hard to imagine the journey began with no hint of the marvels to come.

When I woke the morning of November 1 about 8 a.m., I went into the living room. Outside I saw a beautiful, warm November day. Sheri lay in the Hospice hospital bed, her eyes closed, mouth shut.

Odd, I thought. I remembered her awake and alert the day before as she visited with her step-sister and a long-time friend.

I even looked forward to the afternoon, when we expected a special visitor to arrive. In the early 2000s, we hosted foreign students while they attended college in Irvine. A few of them stayed several years. Takayo and Tomoko, two Japanese sisters, became like daughters to us over the years they shared our house. The day before, a surprise email arrived from Takayo. Her mother heard about Sheri's illness and they planned to fly in from Tokyo to visit.

Denise Lamonte, who spent the previous night with Sheri, stood beside the bed.

She looked up when I walked into the room. "A few minutes ago," she said, "Sheri told me, 'I am going now.' Then she closed her eyes and went to sleep."

I sat by the bed and held her hand. After two rough weeks, she looked exhausted. She had seen everyone she wanted to see. She made her wishes clear to us: "When the time comes, I don't want to linger. I want to close my eyes and leave."

We've all heard of cases where patients, in their last moments, say goodbye and leave within seconds. At first, she looked peaceful, her eyes closed as if she knew her time to leave had arrived. I dreaded the thought of this moment day after day as the year after her diagnosis of inoperable pancreatic cancer passed. I could not bear her loss but I also wanted her to find peace and relief from her intense pain and frustration.

The more I sat with her, the more I realized she didn't look asleep. I sensed tense agitation. Her clenched mouth and tight-shut eyes told me she was making a considerable effort to leave, with no success. When her cat Chico jumped on the bed and pawed at her arm, she reacted with irritation. We saw no danger she would slip away yet.

From six months' perspective, I now see this as the first hint that Sheri's passing would not be normal. Forces we did not sense or understand worked to send her in a different direction. All of us missed the hint.

I showered, dressed and checked my email, where I found another message from Takayo. They would land at Los Angeles Airport about 1 p.m. and drive down to Orange County. I replied, "You can come but I don't know if she will be able to talk to you."

I told Denise about the visit.

"Sheri is sleeping easier," she said. "I'll watch her. Why don't you go out for breakfast? It will do you good."

I always eat breakfast at home but I agreed with her. I had taken care of Sheri 24-7 for 11 months. I needed a break so I went to Ruby's and ate a stack of pancakes. Lots of fat and very good! Just the splurge I needed.

The sad moment of her passing now raced toward us. Her inoperable pancreatic cancer stole the limited time we had with her. I watched her fade over the previous two months, in great pain and discomfort, but still she held on, received visitors and saw old friends and her few relatives, until her energy gave out. Then she ate less, and medications became more difficult to administer.

I and a small group of friends, Alice, Sherree Jolly, and Susan Leone, operated in medical mode. Yes, a Hospice nurse came in three times a week but most of the time we, mostly me, made the decisions. We concentrated on a few tasks, kept her as comfortable as possible and made sure her pain medication was administered, even at three in the morning. We had little guidance as to what to do and how to do it. Each day she responded less and now it looked like she had slipped into unconsciousness for good. The end neared.

Each night for the previous week we had awakened her for her early morning pain pills, with ever greater difficulty. When she could no longer swallow pills, we substituted liquid morphine, which she hated, given with a small syringe in her mouth.

This Sunday morning found us tired and frustrated. Few nurses worked weekends. Denise told us she figured out she didn't need to wake Sheri to give her the morphine dose so we congratulated ourselves on one small victory.

You get the idea. To all of us Sheri's would be a classic passage from this life, with family and friends around her as we watched her weaken and let go in the days to come.

I have a whole list of what we did as the day passed, all the medications we gave her, the moments when she groaned or in a moment of lucidity requested juice, but I won't go into the details here. She no longer talked much and slept most of the time. Even with the morphine we gave her, she still experienced pain much of the time. She also needed Ativan, an anti-anxiety medication, but could no longer swallow the pills.

Around noon, Sheri's friend Jean Wright came by and sang to her for a while. She responded well and for a time calmed down. Another friend, Dave Sullenger, sat with her for an hour or so but she never responded to him.

Then Takayo and her mother arrived for their visit about 3:30 p.m. Through most of the afternoon, I feared they would only be able to sit beside her in silence. However, when the doorbell rang, I noticed Sheri move a bit. When they came in, she raised up and said, "Who is it?"

When I told her, she responded with delight. They talked for a while even with Sheri's slurred speech. They even called Takayo's sister Tomoko in Taiwan and Sheri spoke with her for a few minutes on the phone. She became tired again as I chatted with Takayo and her mother, who left about five. Then Sheri asked to talk to me. I don't remember what she said but when we finished she relapsed into her semi-conscious state.

Because her condition continued to deteriorate, we called for a Hospice nurse, who arrived about 5:30. She showed us how to crush the Ativan and give it to Sheri with liquid by syringe in her mouth. Once she took the medication, she looked much more comfortable and relaxed.

It's hard to get across how strange this felt at the time. An unstoppable force swept us along a path we did not understand. We knew Sheri would not last long but we also knew the next hours and days would be difficult since we had limited professional support from a nurse who visited three times a week. How could we manage medications with her condition in constant flux? The overnight stays exhausted my friends and I knew they couldn't take much more.

We watched Sheri, who said she wanted to be gone from this world right now yet hung on to the edge of eternity, sleep on her bed. All our efforts went to make her body comfortable and pain free.

Often the mind can get locked into a paradigm to the exclusion of all else. We missed the soul, which yearned for our attention, while we fed the body's needs. I am still amazed it took three days for this message to get through.

In mid-afternoon, Susan and Alice, who planned to spend the night, arrived. Alice would stay up until 3 a.m. Monday, then wake Susan, who, as a morning person, went to bed early. Between them, they would take care of the medical duties.

As I went to bed I wondered how long this process would take. To me, no medical professional, it looked like hesitation from Sheri. The classic signs I knew had not yet shown up. It concerned me. If this went on much longer, we would burn out Sheri's friends, who volunteered to stay up all night to take care of her while I got much needed sheep.

It felt strange to expect Sheri's imminent passage but to have no idea what it meant.

What would Monday bring?

TWO

The Beginning of the End, Part 2, January to May 2014

2014 was to be our best year ever.

Sheri wrote every day to finish her new book, *How to Manage Your Hispanic Workforce*, which would establish her as an expert corporate consultant who trained managers to understand and work with their Hispanic workforces. I loved her excitement at her plans to market her services to major corporations who needed what she provided.

My partner Jim Turrell and I had just moved our CSL Writers Workshop online, ready to train professionals to write books that change people's lives.

In January, Sheri and I attended an event, Play to Win, created by Clinton Swaine. I had seen Clinton speak in November and December. He impressed me, but not enough to attend the three-day event he produced, Play to Win. I hung out with his assistant Bokkie a few times after the talks and she convinced me to attend in January in Los Angeles. I called Sheri and invited her as well.

I am not an event junkie. I promoted a large multi-speaker event, Speak Your Way to Wealth, for six years and was not impressed enough with most of the people I met to join their programs. From experience, I knew free events led to sales pitches.

Sheri and I attended but given our shaky financial position, we had no money to spend on expensive programs.

I already knew Clinton as an expert speech and business trainer. When we walked into the room at the Los Angeles Convention Center with about 60 other people I sensed this would be different. After I walked up on stage at the start to introduce myself, he coached me for about 10 minutes and later told me he wanted to work with me.

I won't go into the details of the training since it might spoil the experience should you decide to attend one in the future (which I recommend). I noticed only one discordant note. Sheri looked uncomfortable in the metal folding chairs and mentioned back pain a few times. At the end of one of the most emotional experiences I have ever had, Sheri and I made a deal with Clinton and became part of Frontier Trainings. Two days later, we attended our first three advanced courses in San Diego. We left excited about the new future we saw open before us.

Valentine's Day in the Emergency Room

When illness strikes, the first inclination is to not believe the obvious. The round of doctors, hospitals and emergency rooms becomes a blur of nonsense. The experts' words do not compute -- test, operation, biopsy, malignant, tumor, rest, diet, benign, pill, medicate. They cannot describe us or our condition, not mine and for certain not my wife's.

I remember the first, not even noticeable, start of our journey, the small complaint of back pain while we sat in the training room at Play to Win. The final, greatest challenge of Sheri's life began in the same moment we embraced our apparent bright business future at an age when most people think of retirement.

A bit of pain in the back is normal when you sit in uncomfortable chairs for hours. It happens all the time. After we returned from San Diego in late January 2014, I didn't notice when Sheri went to our chiropractor for the pain. She had back problems and visited him often. Routine. She came home with no comment. Next morning, she still had a sore back. Still not a big deal. Soreness happened. We dealt with it before. I heard an occasional complaint and heard about another visit to the chiro with the same non-results. He called it a twisted hip.

When it didn't improve after a couple of days, she said, "Jerry will look at it." Jerry, a retired chiropractor in his mid-80s, dated Sheri's friend Joy. He had a reputation: he could fix back problems, so we heard. One glance and he saw the problem. "Twisted pelvis," he said. Same diagnosis as the other chiro. "Never found one I couldn't fix," he said. He adjusted her and we went home. The pain didn't go away.

By early February, Sheri became frustrated when the pain refused to ease. It showed up, better or worse on certain days, but persistent. It became the barometer of success, pain=failure, no pain=the medication worked. So far, no magic bullets. The pain proved so uncomfortable we went to Dr. Granlund February 3. She ordered a spine x-ray. No problems. Sheri returned to her office Friday and again the next Wednesday with no real answers.

Two days passed, a lot of Ibuprofen got downed and Valentine's Day arrived. We planned a nice early dinner, not fancy, but pleasant. Many Valentine's dinners are huge profit opportunities for the restaurant industry (pay $75 for the same meal you can eat tomorrow for $9.50). We preferred fun and romance to big tickets and sizzling candles.

But first we went to a doctor's appointment at 2 p.m. Sheri asked Dr. Granlund about the pain, which refused to away but got worse. First the doctor ordered an ultrasound. This uncomfortable procedure showed no problems. Dr. Granlund then told Sheri she needed a CAT scan but to schedule one could take days or weeks and we didn't want to wait. The answer? A visit to the emergency room, where they do CAT scans right away. Sheri agreed, "I can't stand this. Let's do it."

In this moment, I stepped into unfamiliar territory. My experience with emergency rooms consisted of a few episodes of the TV series ER years ago. I remember George Clooney and Julianna Margulies and a lot of chaos. I had never seen a real ER so no experience prepared me for it.

When Sheri's illness hit, I had no idea what to do. Without experience, I didn't know the questions to ask, how the medical system worked, or what symptoms to look for. How could I help Sheri if I had no clue as to the nature of the problem? What a scary prospect.

To understand how weird the situation felt, I last visited a hospital when my tonsils came out at the age of 12. I remember I chewed on a few ice cubes before we headed for home.

To me, other people ended up in the hospital, not ones I knew. Saddleback Hospital, one of the best in Orange County, sat five minutes from home. We liked the intellectual satisfaction but never expected to visit it so soon. I had no idea what went on inside those walls.

When we walked into the emergency room about 4 p.m. on Valentine's Day 2014, 57 years after the tonsils came out, I thought, "So this is what an emergency room looks like." Not like TV, more sedate, an empty waiting room. The deliberate pace surprised me.

Outside, the Valentine's Day rush to spend money on dinners proceeded in full march. Cars eased into parking lots and disgorged men in serious suits and women in fancy dresses decked out with lots of roses.

Inside, the nurse at the desk checked Sheri's insurance, printed out a wristband and asked the two questions, a mantra we encountered every time we visited a new doctor or nurse: "What is your name?" "What is your date of birth?"

They ushered us in to see the triage nurse within minutes. A few moments later, we settled into a curtained room in the bowels of the ER, 30 rooms with several corridors and two nurses' stations where the nurses hung out.

My first impression: A place full of doctors of all kinds, more doctors than patients, like an expedition into an unknown land peopled by alien life forms.

Sheri changed into the requisite hospital gown and the nurses hooked her up to monitors, which buzzed and beeped as they collected vital signs. The nurses attached an IV drip, a blood pressure cup to her arm, a clothespin with a red light to her finger, and put her in a rollaway hospital bed.

We waited.

Outside, the emergency room felt dead. A few nurses wandered about.

Doctors, identifiable by white coats of a certain length, flitted by.

We waited.

"The doctor will be by soon," the nurse said. She failed to define "soon," an all-purpose word I later decided meant "at an undetermined time tonight."

We waited.

Five p.m. came and went, then six. I got hungry. I chatted with Sheri but we didn't have much to say. After a while, she called a friend to bring me dinner (the nurses wouldn't let her eat). I expected a simple dinner but the prospect of a burrito while seated on a hard chair with no table in the Saddleback emergency room sounded way too simple.

After a few hours, the doctor showed up. When informed she had back pain, he reassured us, "We get a lot of people with back pain and often we never figure it out." He ordered a CAT scan and went away.

We waited.

About 8 p.m., a couple of guys showed up and wheeled Sheri off to the CAT scan room, where I could not go. After half an hour, they wheeled her back.

We waited again, this time for the doctor to show up and give us the results.

After another hour, the doctor returned to give us a clear diagnosis. "I have no idea of the cause of the pain," he said. "In most cases, it goes away after a while." We chatted for a few minutes, then he added, as an afterthought, "By the way, the radiologist saw a mass on the adrenal gland. You should get it checked."

He smiled and left. The hospital staff unhooked all the wires and tubes and sent us on our way about 10 p.m.

Frustration. No conclusive answer. It is always better to know than to not know. Frustration with the system that provides such indeterminate answers is why so many people give up on medicine. Yet with a complex system like the human body, answers aren't easy. In the back of my mind, and maybe Sheri's, lurked the possibility a serious illness might hide behind this innocuous backache. Neither of us brought up the possibility and neither did the doctors.

Our lives were about to change forever.

The Search for an Answer

The medical profession went into high gear. I won't go into all the details because they aren't relevant. Sheri had back pain and she had an adrenal mass. We guessed they might be connected.

In short order, Sheri had another CAT scan, had a mammogram, saw the upper GI doctor, the oncologist, a urologist, and a surgeon. After a biopsy, the oncologist revealed the results. Sheri had a pheochromocytoma tumor in her left adrenal gland.

You are not alone if you never heard of this critter. Even most doctors have no idea what it is. Less than 20,000 cases per year show up in the whole country. This insidious tumor sprays random shots of adrenaline into the body, which can cause all kinds of dangerous reactions. The good news? A benign tumor. No cancer.

"I am amazed we caught it," Dr. Wagner, the oncologist, told us. "The first symptom is often either a stroke, heart attack, or death."

We breathed a collective sigh of relief and scheduled the surgery for May 21, 2014 with the only Orange County doctor who did them and had only done 10 of them in the past year. That's how rare this critter was.

The laparoscopic surgery succeeded. Sheri left the hospital with four inch-long incisions. They healed fast. She spent the rest of May in recovery and went back to work with her therapy clients. We could get on with our lives.

Except for a pesky bit of back pain that refused to go away.

THREE

The End of the Beginning, April 1993 to July 1996

As I write this, it is Christmas morning 2015. Sheri loved Christmas and I am sure she knows I am invited to two or three celebrations of her favorite holiday later this afternoon. One of my cats sits on my lap like he does most days. Sheri passed and ended the earthly portion of our marriage about a month and a half ago. I still wear the wedding ring she gave me so many years ago. It may not be time to let go but I know the time will come soon.

However, I will never let go of the memories of the great times we had together. As you relive them with me over the course of this book, think about her adventurous spirit, which first showed up in my life so many years ago.

She also loved other holidays and celebrations. She put on parties any time or place. When one of her friends, Marlene Beno, decided to get married, she volunteered to help. Later Sheri told me the wedding excited her for a couple of reasons, first, of course, her friend was the bride. But second, she was on a 20-year quest to find a soulmate.

Marlene planned to marry Jack Charron, a friend of mine for the past two years and a fellow member of Sol Stein's Chapter One writers group. He invited a bunch of us from the group to his wedding.

The small, festive wedding took place on April 3, 1993 in the back yard of their home in Irvine, California, a few blocks away from my home at the time. About 50 people came to see the bride and groom marry.

Now, to be clear, I did not want a relationship. I had divorced my previous wife a few years earlier and spent my time on novels and work in Beverly Hills, California as Chief Financial Officer for Beverly Hills [213], a society magazine. The novels led me to meet Sol, one of the top New York publishers of the 20th century, which led to my presence at this wedding.

I never noticed Sheri as the wedding proceeded. At the reception, I chatted with my friends and with Jack and Marlene. Then the traditional reception events unwound in the usual order. We had the toast, the bride and groom cut the cake and then came time for the bouquet and garter tosses.

I never saw the bouquet. Later Sheri told me Marlene looked around the yard and told Sheri, "I don't see many single women here." She handed the bouquet to Sheri (which again I never saw). "Here, it's yours," she said.

Then Jack took his turn. A bunch of us gathered around him, among them several from the writing group. Jack slipped the garter off Marlene's leg and turned his back. I stood off to one side and as he tossed it over his shoulder it sailed right towards me. I reached forward and grabbed it.

Wow, I thought. Never caught one of those before. Then I felt a tap on the shoulder and turned. A woman about my age dressed as a bridesmaid with a bouquet of flowers in her hands stood in front of me, a smile on her face. "I got the bouquet," she said. "Let's check this out."

We started to talk and the wedding celebration faded into the background. I have no idea how long it went on but when the party wound down we were still talking. One of my friends, Steve Talsky, said he approached us once but found us so oblivious to the rest of the party he went away. I had discovered a new friend who felt like an old friend I had missed for a long time.

When we parted, we exchanged phone numbers.

Coincidence or ...

When I called her the next day, she invited me to a church social at her house on Saturday. Such a first date might cause a problem because religion is very personal and can stop a relationship before it gets started. However, in our lengthy conversation at the wedding, it became clear we both shared the same religious philosophy, Science of Mind, based on the teachings of Ernest Holmes.

This isn't a commercial for you to check it out (might be nice though) but to point out how many coincidences influence our life events. When I look back on the number of choices I made (and she made) on the road to Jack and Marlene's wedding, it staggers the mind. The same is true of your life. One different step 10 years earlier and life goes in a different direction.

Anyway, I went to the party, enjoyed myself, learned about Jim Turrell's church in Costa Mesa, California, and started to attend with Sheri. One of the first couples I met, Sherree and

Dave Jolly, became great friends. Sherree shared a spiritual mastermind with Sheri and joined the team that guided Sheri through the last nine days of her life.

Over the next several months, we dated off and on, then more and more. We spent time at her condo in Orange and my house in Irvine as we got to know each other. I remember she shared a lot about her childhood in Yuma, Arizona and the negative affect it left on her.

When I told her about my family, how they never put my sister and me down, how they supported us, never got negative with us, traveled with us, and so forth, she refused to believe my story of a good childhood. Then she met my parents and realized they were the close family she yearned for but never experienced.

We started to talk marriage in August (she did most of the talking at first) and by September we decided to tie the knot. Now this may be odd but we made the decision and then I proposed to her. The decision satisfied me but she needed a moment of formal traditional ritual to seal the decision.

Wedding Bells

Sheri was a party girl. No simple courthouse ceremony for her. It took seven months to put the party together.

We had to dance, Sheri said, so we took swing dance lessons and choreographed our entry, a dance into the reception hall.

In those days, I wore glasses because of nearsightedness. In April, she talked me into a visit to the optometrist to fit me with contact lenses. "You will look so much better," she said. I went along with it and got the new contacts the Friday before the wedding. The difference in vision and comfort amazed me. As usual, she called it. I never went back to glasses.

Sheri had to arrive in style so we enlisted her friend Yvette, who owned a 70's era Rolls Royce, for the drive to the wedding.

We spent days on the search for the best venue and food. We had a budget so we didn't want to go over the top expensive. After we checked out several locations, we settled on the perfect place, the El Adobe Restaurant in San Juan Capistrano, an old adobe built under Spanish colonial rule turned into a delightful Mexican restaurant. The outdoor patio could seat over two hundred people and had a beautiful altar area where the ceremony would take place. Inside, the circular reception area's roof opened to admit lots of California sunshine.

May 1, 1994 dawned cloudy and windy with chilly temperatures, not the best weather for an outdoor wedding. As the morning progressed, the clouds cleared up, the sun came out and the temperature rose. By one p.m. over a hundred people had gathered in the patio ready for us to say our vows.

The wedding party, Yvette, Pam, Sheri, Lee, Jim Turrell, Ray Pound

My dad Ray Pound served as my best man and Yvette and Pam, her step-sister, acted as bridesmaids. We did all the traditional rites, the march down the aisle, tuxes, a white wedding dress, her step-father gave her away, a big cake, the bouquet and garter toss (no new romance though), and a big party with a deejay, music, and lots of tasty Mexican food and dancing, dancing, dancing.

After hours of celebration, we went to our house in Irvine to get ready for our honeymoon trip. About 8:30 p.m. the phone rang. Her uncle Howard Rehme said his doctor had just told him he had cancer and had only a few months to live.

On that somber note, we went to bed. Early the next morning, we drove to Phoenix, Arizona and picked up the keys to a private mountain cabin owned by her high school girlfriend, Gale Ekiss.

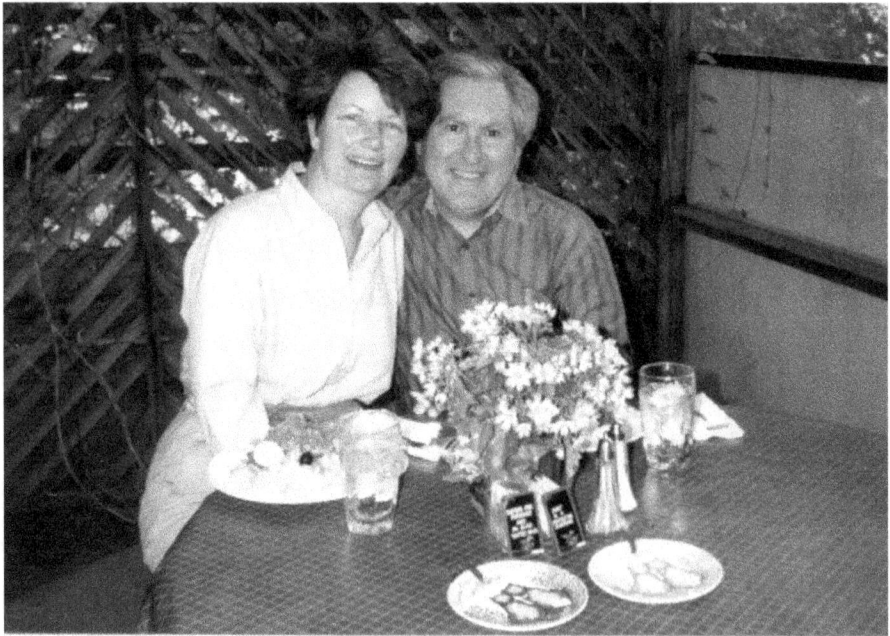

Sheri and Lee on honeymoon, Tonto Village, Arizona, May 1994

We spent a week in the cabin, near Payson, Arizona. We hung out, painted, drove around, hiked, and rested after the ordeal of such a big wedding. We brought our own food, among it a large glass baking dish of garlic mashed potatoes. Sheri loved garlic but she admitted she had added a bit too much so we laughed about the hot potatoes for the rest of our honeymoon. What a wonderful opportunity to get to know each other even better, to relax and to talk about our new life together.

Houses, houses and more houses.

Sheri had moved into my house and rented out her condo in Orange after we decided to get married in September. Although I found it adequate, the 1,100-square-foot condo on Seton Road in Irvine proved a tight fit for both of us. We split my office in two (and got rid of my rocking chair) and stumbled over each other quite a bit while we spent the next six months on the wedding.

After we got home from the honeymoon in mid-May 1994, we decided to find a larger house so we could both have a private office. We both made good money at the time and with a third house to live in and two rentals we started on our way to a new status as property barons.

We looked at quite a few places in University Park, one of the more affordable sections of Irvine, and Sheri fell in love with a house two blocks away on Ash Tree Lane, which had two stories and three bedrooms, plenty of room for two offices, parties, and guests. We made an offer and opened escrow on June 28, 1994.

In the middle of plans to move down the street, we got a call from Reno, Nevada on July 27. Sheri's uncle Howard was in the hospital with the terminal cancer he told us about after the wedding. Howard was Sheri's last living full-blood relative. I met him when we visited him in Quincy, California, a tiny mountain town near Reno, late in 1993. He served as a bomber pilot and flew 80 or more missions over Europe in World War II. Sheri said he never talked much about the war but knew it had affected him deeply. Other than a brief marriage in 1957, he had lived a bachelor's life in Quincy.

As soon as the call came in, we hit the road in hopes we could get to Reno before he passed away. In the early morning hours of July 28, near Modesto, we got a call. He had passed. Sheri broke into tears. We pulled into Reno as daylight broke across the eastern horizon to make the necessary arrangements.

Later, we drove to Quincy, about two hours away, to check out his house. Over the next few days, we cleared the house out and prepared it for rental. Now we owned three houses and our fourth would close escrow August 26, 1994.

In September we moved, settled into our new home, and rented out my condo. The wonderful new house had plenty of room for both of us and our offices.

Honeymoon Number Two

In the summer of 1995, our church held a fund-raiser auction. We discovered the big prize: two airline tickets to Paris, France. We looked at each other then back at our two weeks in the Arizona mountains, and said, "Let's do another honeymoon to Paris and do it right this time!" (Okay, Sheri had the idea.)

One problem. We still had to win the tickets. The night of the auction arrives and we show up, the newlyweds who want a romantic getaway. Who else would bid against us? Turned out one showed up, a good friend who flew to Europe at times.

We bid.

He bid.

We bid.

He bid.

By the time it got to $800 we wondered how far to carry this. We hissed at to him to stop his bids and the audience got restless because most of them knew what this meant to us. Then, with the price at $800, he stood up, looked at us, shook his head, and sat back down. We won the trip.

Now we had to figure out what to do with it. We didn't have to go right away so Sheri started to think about what to do in France.

Servas

As we started preparations for the trip, scheduled for July 1996, Sheri said, "I don't want to stay in hotels."

What a second introduction to Sheri's unique way of living. At first, I agreed we might be able to find other accommodations. (I didn't know what she had in mind.) We talked often about her interest in other cultures but I saw most of her interest as Mexican culture.

"No," she said. "What's the best way to learn about another culture? Live with them!" She handed me a brochure. "Look at this program I heard about."

Servas? I'd never heard of the organization. The brochure said it facilitated home stays in countries all over the world to build international relationships and world peace. To use it, we needed to sign up, pay a small fee, and be interviewed by a local member to see if we qualified for the program.

The interview with the local member, who lived in Newport Beach, went fast. They wanted people like us, a stable middle-class couple who wanted to meet interesting people. The interviewer stamped our application and we ordered the book listing the hosts who lived in France.

When it came, we paged through it. Sheri's excitement grew as she discovered the hundreds of families, most of whom spoke English, who wanted visitors. The simple next steps? Plan our itinerary, decide who we wanted to stay with and call them up and ask if we could stay those dates. The only rule? Spend two nights with each family to get acquainted with the culture of their region.

This turned into one of those adventures only Sheri could come up with. You can't buy a vacation like this. It is not for sale anywhere.

"Of course, we'll speak French when we go to France," she said. I knew she spoke no French but near perfect Spanish. These two Latin-based languages had similar grammar and word roots. I wouldn't be hard for her to learn French.

"I took two years in high school," I said. I could still read French but couldn't speak it now.

"They've got French classes at Irvine Valley College," she said. (She'd checked into this before we talked.) "I want to learn it. They say it's a lot like Spanish."

"Except in Spanish they pronounce all the letters and in French they pronounce very few of them."

We decided to take the classes. My French came back within a few months. Sheri learned fast over the next two semesters, from September 1995 to June 1996, but spoke with a Spanish accent. We would finish the last class and fly out to France within a week.

While we studied French, Sheri called French families and received an ecstatic welcome from everyone she talked to. Most lived in rural towns, which attracted few visitors, so they welcomed our request to stay with them. Within a few days, we lined up seven families ready to host us. One, near Paris, needed to confirm later but the rest were solid.

After we chose our hosts, we constructed our itinerary. We would start in Paris for four or five days, then rent a car and drive to Alençon in Normandy, an old lace-making town, Brittany, Amboise, a chateau town in the Loire Valley, Toulouse and east to Lyons and back to Paris.

July came and we boarded the plane from Los Angeles to Paris. The airline bumped us up to business class so we sat beside a French family on their way to Paris from Samoa. (He was Samoan.)

We chatted for a while and Sheri mentioned our plans to stay with families. "Our last family hasn't responded yet," Sheri added.

They said, "If you don't hear from them, give us a call and you can stay with us!"

It turned out they lived in Etampes, 30 kilometers from Paris, perfect for our last stop.

The trip amazed us. We spent six days in Paris, three of them in small hotels and three in a penthouse apartment on Rue Henri IV near the Bastille across from the military academy. We saw Notre Dame, the famous Shakespeare and Company bookstore, Versailles and Fontainebleau, and rode the Metro all over Paris.

In Alençon, we stayed with a family who ran a nursery business, spent two days with a family on the coast of Brittany, two days with a pair of nurses in Amboise, three days in the village of Montferran west of Toulouse, a night in Conques, a beautiful mountain village little changed since the Middle Ages, a couple of nights with a couple in Aurillac, who taught us how to make a fun dish of potatoes and cheese called aligot, and in a small hotel in Thiers, the knife-making capital of France since the 14th century. And yes, we stayed with the family in Etampes we met on the plane before we flew home.

What a way to start a marriage!

Tranquility abounds in the Universe. All is calm, cool and collected. Me too because obviously I'm part of Universe. I move confidently through the day achieving much more than I imagined possible because I'm calm, cool, and collected and confident in my competency. Thank you! Thank you! Thank You! I let go and enjoy the flow.
Sheri Long
October 21, 2012

FOUR

The Beginning,
Part 1
March 1948 to 1973

The more I heard the story of Sheri's youth, which emerged in bits and pieces over the first year we knew each other, the more I wondered how the fun-loving woman I knew could have come from such an awful childhood.

First, you must understand I had no benchmark by which to judge her story and she had none to judge mine. My parents were as good as one could ask for. My dad, Ray Pound, a professional photographer, worked for himself most of his life. In their chosen home town of Placentia, the voters elected him mayor when the city began to grow. Both were active in the Presbyterian Church.

My mother supported him in his endeavors and gave my sister and me unquestioned support in our endeavors. We both won the top student trophy in our high school classes two years in a row. They stayed married for 56 years, until he passed away, and lived in the same house in Placentia, California for 49 of those years. After 62 years in the family, my sister and I sold it in 2011. I can still drive by when I want and see the old family home. Placentia, the quintessential small-town American city, consisted of about 2,000 people nestled in the orange groves. We knew everyone in town. My high school class graduated 97 students, all of us friends.

When we first met, I told Sheri about this, to me, most normal childhood in the world. She refused to believe me until she met and experienced my family and even then, she suspected hidden darkness behind the façade of good relations. It took a while, but in the end, she accepted my family's welcome embrace and saw my parents as the mother and father she wished she had.

As she revealed her story, which I will go into detail in a moment, I came to better understand her childhood as like an orphan with parents. Her references to alcohol, divorce, the put-downs, and her loneliness made sense. I had heard about others with such experiences and the effect it had on their lives.

Since I worked in publishing and the self-help industry, I had heard scattered horror stories of bad childhoods so I understood it could happen.

She never told the whole story to me but referred at times to various incidents. I got a picture of an unhappy young girl who grew up in a toxic environment. I even wrote many of the sections of this chapter from this knowledge. Still, I wondered what I had missed.

As we got to know each other better, more of the story emerged. I knew she had a master's degree and soon found out its subject: alcohol rehabilitation. She enjoyed her job as an

Employee Assistance Professional, where she did marriage and family therapy for corporate employees. I soon learned she had spent years in therapy herself and had joined an alcoholism support group for adult children of alcoholics. Any thought of drinking turned her off. Serious stuff. Yet on first meeting her, you saw a happy, fun-loving woman who threw lots of parties, had so many close friends you couldn't count them, loved Christmas, and exuded generosity. She also spoke Spanish better than many Mexicans. She had an innate gift for making connections with a few words.

She had a darker side as well. She was single for over 20 years, with one relationship after another and no commitment to anyone. She never made much money and was less than successful in her therapy business. Although smart, she doubted her own abilities and took few risks. She refused to tolerate friends who didn't pay a lot of attention to her and even broke up with at least two close friends because of this. At times she would criticize people, and me at times as well, with an uncharacteristic roughness.

We also shared a strong antipathy to organized religion and common membership in the Church of Religious Science. This non-denominational philosophy incorporates aspects of all the major religious traditions, both east and west, with minimal dogma. I think three basics drew her to it: it emphasized positive thoughts, it said we as individuals control our destiny through our thoughts, and it welcomed people of all faiths into its fold with no demands.

When I learned both her parents were alcoholics, her actions became clearer. She called Willa, her mother, a very bad drunk who never gave up alcohol. She also recalled numerous times when Willa would put her down without mercy, called her dumb, stupid, never a success, and worse. She called it such a horrible psychological mess she could not stand to go home after school. Home resembled a harsh prison more than a safe refuge.

Worse yet, she grew up alone. As an only child, she had no brothers and sisters to play with. And even worse, she lived 10 miles south of Yuma on date ranch two miles from the Mexican border. Empty sand stretched away in all directions. She often escaped into the desert for a favorite activity, to catch lizards and other desert creatures among the silent expanses beyond her house. Only school and two families who became her families away from home broke into this lonely life.

This sums up what I knew about her childhood while she lived. Then a couple of days ago, while I cleaned out and sorted Sheri's books, I came across notes on her years from age 4 to 6. As I read what she wrote, I saw how her family had affected her, how much pain they had inflicted and how they made her home life unsafe.

She wrote these notes five years ago at the age of 62. In them I saw the unvarnished truth of a life that still reeled from incidents 60 years in the past.

I noticed the letters ETOH scattered through her notes. It is a term I had never seen before so a few minutes ago I looked it up on the Internet. No surprise when I saw it referred to alcohol and could also mean "extremely trashed or hammered," according to one website definition. With her master's degree in alcohol rehabilitation and the years she dealt with the pervasive drunken behavior of those around her as a child, the term became second nature to her.

In the notes, I saw the hurt young pre-teen girl, able to remember little of her early life, talk about a horrible mother who terrified her, a father who vanished, and friendlessness all around. I can't imagine how much she had to heal from those years.

On Willa, she wrote two paragraphs, one positive and one negative. I will let them speak for themselves.

Positive: Willa was "Smart, fun sense of humor, playful, wanted one daughter, let me choose religion, told me I could do anything, funded education, supported abortion, pretty, cared about my friends, loved me, vacations, pets, stayed in touch when married, loved Sam (her dog), taught me how to dress."

Negative: Willa was "Critical, alkie, selfish, controlling, unhappy, relied on me/told me adult problems when 7-12, called me suicidal, had sex in the room next to my bedroom, took me to bars, criticized me in front of teacher, peers, etc., smoked, against black husband, obsesses with money and possessions, wouldn't share food, discouraged art, restricted."

Then I found a story from age four in a note about family, "Willa said 'Don't call me Mommy.' I asked her name, which I called her forever." Even decades after her mother died, she still called her Willa, as if the name "Mommy" remained forbidden.

Then she wrote about her environment, her home on the 40-acre date ranch. Positive: Nature, huge back yard, pets, Cruz, we built house, pool fun, farm and Mexican workers, desert.

Negative: 8 miles away from town, scary, depressing prison, trapped, no way out, abusive, no food, sex, fighting, cold, alone, defenseless, oppressive, stifling my spirit, fear of neighbor's sexual advances."

This is a difficult chapter to read and even more difficult to write but I put in a lot of detail since these years and the psychological damage they did make her last days on earth understandable.

A Dysfunctional Family

Sheri was born in Los Angeles, California, March 31, 1948 to Bill and Willa Long. Her dad, a real estate developer, had two older children who lived with his ex-wife in northern California. Her mother married in her early 20s but it did not last and she soon divorced him. After she married Bill, they lived in Glendale, California for her first four years, which she said she didn't remember, then her father moved the family to Arizona in 1952, first to Phoenix.

In all these notes, she defined her physical health as "great." She told three stories about this first home in Phoenix at age 4, which made a great impression on her.

The first is about a swimming race in a backyard pool. She said her family cheered her on but she stopped the race before an imminent finish in first place. "Maybe I wanted to be accepted by the other kids," she noted.

Another time, she played near a pile of cut open plant cans even though her mother told her not to play with them. She cut her elbow on one of them. "They took me to the hospital to get a shot," she wrote. "Bill drove, Willa held me crying in the car and during the shot. Willa told me everyone heard my screams in the hospital."

By Easter, the family moved to a nicer house on a paved street with a pool and lawn. For Easter, her mother forgot the

Easter egg dyes so she painted birds on her eggs. "Then," she wrote, "my neighbors took me to the Easter egg hunt. I didn't understand and wanted the special eggs my Mom painted. I cried until I got them. Her special attention seemed so scarce I didn't dare lose any of it."

Often, when adults visited the house, her parents would put her in her room. "I felt like they punished me for being me. Banished. Not important. Not approved or loved."

Her mother also forbade her to visit the neighbor's bunnies. "The neighbor welcomed me to hold the bunnies," she said. "He didn't seem bothered by my enthusiastic presence like my mom said he would be if I visited as often as I wanted. I felt I wasn't good enough, a bother, nuisance, unworthy."

In 1953, Bill and Willa moved into a cute apartment behind a big house near Orange Avenue in old downtown Yuma, Arizona. She started first grade in downtown Yuma in the fall. "I don't remember being sad to leave Phoenix," she wrote. "I don't recall any friendships."

Then Bill bought a date farm called Persian Gardens, ten miles south of Yuma, and built a house on the property. Sheri grew up in this house, her real home, which she expected to inherit from her parents. I remember how special she considered it when we first visited Yuma in 1993. This home was her history, her past.

She transferred to Somerton Grammar School in the middle of first grade. She often repeated her early memories where she "walked all over the ranch and desert catching lizards." Her parents built their new house together and often received visits from her grandparents and uncle Howard.

In these early years, both Bill and Willa worked. Bill stayed home most of the time. They had cows and a horse.

She also mentioned country club parties and daily drinking.

Willa, Sheri, and Bill about 1956, Yuma Arizona

In 1955, when she was 7, Bill took a sales job in California and brought gifts home from his travels. By 1959, Bill "was gone most of the time in California. I loved it when he returned. Willa confided in me that Bill has girlfriends and not much money and might move to San Francisco."

Also in 1959, she wrote, "A teacher took me into the classroom's bathroom, told me he loved me, hugged me, maybe more?"

On July 28, 1960, just after Sheri turned 12, Bill and Willa divorced. The divorce "ended the struggle," Sheri wrote. "It was the beginning of Hell with Willa's reactionary drinking (ETOH) and sex." Her father remarried in Riverside, California two days later, July 30, 1960.

He became a real estate developer in Orange County, California when the development boom hit in the early 1960s, served as president of the Orange County Chapter of the Building Contractors Association of California in 1965, owned Four Seasons Homes and W. G. Long Construction Company, and joined Dike & Colgrove of Costa Mesa in 1965. He built residential tracts in Fountain Valley and nearby cities and became wealthy enough to buy a house on Lido Island in Newport Beach, a few miles from our home in Irvine.

When we would go to Newport, she would often have me drive out to Lido Island to show me the house Bill Long owned and where she spent many fun vacation days as a teenager.

Salvador, Cruz and Learning Spanish

Sheri and Cruz

Cruz and Salvador arrived on the date ranch in 1954, when Sheri turned six. They lived across the border in the dusty Mexican town of San Luis Rio Colorado. Salvador became her father's ranch supervisor and Cruz worked in the family home as a maid. Sheri recalls Cruz as a way to escape from her life of deprivation. "The problem was," she told me, "I spoke only English and Cruz spoke only Spanish. I decided to teach her English." She ran to get one of her books and found a picture of a cat. She held it open in front of Cruz and with a smile said, "Cat!" Cruz said, "Gato!" as emphatically. Sheri gave it another try with the same result. "Cat." "Gato." "Cat." "Gato." After a while, it became evident Cruz had no interest in English. "I gave up," Sheri said, "and decided to learn Spanish from Cruz so we could communicate, the best decision I ever made."

Cruz became her best friend. "I spent lots of hours with her," she wrote. "However, Salvador drank a lot." She used the

ETOH term. Four years later, Cruz got deported from the ranch in the middle of Sheri's 10th birthday party. "It ripped my heart out. Huge loss," she wrote. "Now I'm stuck alone with Willa – no buffer to her toxicity. Upset. Tried to get her back. Took a long time."

They remained life-long friends. On one of our first trips together, to Yuma in 1993, we crossed the border to see Cruz and Salvador, who still lived in the same house Sheri knew from her early days. When we walked up to the house, she asked about Cruz and discovered her friend and teacher had passed away a few days earlier. I remember her distress when she realized such a powerful force in her life had left. "Cruz departed. She smoked, and died without me," Sheri wrote.

We later found Salvador and had a great although subdued visit with him. He greeted her like a long-lost best friend and I could see the connection. As we talked he told us how much he missed Cruz. "He was an alkie, stubborn, and didn't want to live without Cruz," she wrote.

About a year later, we learned he had become increasingly depressed and had shot himself in the head in the middle of his living room. Again, this news caused Sheri a lot of distress. Another part of her past gone.

School

Sheri attended elementary school in Somerton, Arizona, the nearest small town. Her report cards show an excellent student. The first card I have, for fourth grade, shows A grades in reading, language and spelling, and B grades in geography and history. Her teacher gave her top marks for interest, preparation and conduct. This pattern shows up later as she loved languages but could never get interested in history or geography and knew little about either when we met many years later. The school, 80 percent Mexican, gave her ample opportunity to practice Spanish. She joined and became president of the Spanish Club. This started her love affair with Mexican culture.

The Callahans

Robert and Pat Callahan lived about a mile north of the Longs on A Street at 17th, closer to Yuma. Their home became her escape. "I spent as much time at their house as I did at home," she said. Bob Callahan had wide-ranging interests and Pat cared for Sheri like a second mother. Pat also worked hard to preserve the history of Yuma. Most times we talked about Yuma, she mentioned them as the one steady rock in her otherwise turbulent life. I met them in the 1990's and they welcomed me like part of the family.

Willa and Harold Ormsby

Sheri continued to live with her mother in Yuma. Willa married Harold W. Ormsby, a local rancher and desert agriculture expert, December 30, 1961 in Riverside, California. He moved into the Persian Gardens house,

Harold became the one bright light in her teenage years. Even as Willa kept up her drunken ways and discouraged her, Harold encouraged her to be her best. A Santa Barbara, California native, he moved to Yuma in 1942 to take up desert farming. When I met him in 1994, I found a taciturn man in his eighties, fascinating to talk with. He had a wide knowledge of history and of agriculture. Even then he still went to work every day in his greenhouse despite two hip replacements. I always enjoyed my talks with him and delighted in his stories of working with Egyptian President Anwar Sadat on desert agriculture in Egypt and travels to Europe. Sheri loved him as the father she wanted as a child and as the last connection to her past. When he died in 2006 at 94 years old, she mourned the loss of the last of her small family.

Around 1963, she met her step-sister, Pamela Ormsby, Harold Ormsby's daughter by his first wife, at the time a precocious nine-year-old, when she came to visit and later live with them in Yuma.

Mexico

She met her lifelong friend Gale Ekiss in elementary school then she attended Kofa High School in Yuma, where she joined the Spanish Club and took part in campus activities. After graduation May 25, 1966, she attended Western Arizona Junior College in Yuma.

Two years later, after she graduated on May 24, 1968, she found a special summer program in Guadalajara, Mexico and enrolled. Harold and Willa traveled to Mexico with her and returned home in June, after the summer program started. She took classes in Drawing, Mexican Folk Dance, Mexican Folk Songs, and Advanced Spanish Conversation.

While in Mexico City she met her life-long friend Yvette, who became a talented long-distance runner. They attended the 1968 Mexico City Olympics together and became like sisters, which neither ever had.

After that summer, she enjoyed the freedom and the culture so much she looked for ways to stay and discovered the University of the Americas in Mexico City. "I was afraid to ask my mother if I could enroll," she said. Her mother surprised her and said, "Yes."

In the fall of 1968, she enrolled in the University of the Americas, a momentous time for her. She now lived 1,600 miles away from her mother, who dominated her life with negativity, in a foreign country where for two years she would make her own decisions. She immersed herself, spoke Spanish outside of class, dated Mexican men, and deepened her lifelong love of Mexican culture.

On August 24, 1969, Sheri flew home to attend the 50th wedding anniversary of her grandparents, William and Winifred Rehme, in Turlock, California. The gift list showed Sheri brought an arrangement of Mexican flowers.

(From newspaper) Howard Rehme, Sheri Long, Winifred and William Rehme, Willa Ormsby

In her senior year, the college moved to Cholula, across the freeway from the city of Puebla. In Puebla, she met and dated one of the Cabrera brothers. "After we had dated for a while, one of his brothers had a son," she remembered. "Because I was almost part of the family, he asked me to be the baby's Godmother." She had no idea what a godmother did. "His wife told me you had to be Catholic and would play a role in raising him," she says. "I ignored the Catholic part and nobody asked so I accepted."

Francisco, or Paco, his nickname, became an integral part of her life. He became the son she never had for herself. He later married and had two children of his own. Again, we visited them in Mexico often in the 1990s and I found them a family who loved and welcomed Sheri. The first time we went south, the entire family, nine of Paco's aunts and uncles, threw a huge barbecue with homemade tamales and delicacies in a local park to welcome us. I could tell all of them loved her and cared for her. Paco's aunt Rocio visited us several times in Irvine.

Her years in Mexico gave her a greater appreciation for the difficult time Mexicans have when they try to integrate into life in the United States because of unappreciated cultural differences. Her deep knowledge of Spanish, which she spoke like a native the rest of her life, became her entry point into a career centered on help for those with severe emotional and substance abuse problems to live better lives. She connected on a deep level with her Mexican clients because they felt she understood them better than anyone else in their lives.

Her unbearable experiences as a child and young woman gave her a powerful understanding of people with psychological problems invaluable to her clients.

A couple of summers around 1970, she went to Mill Valley, California, near San Francisco, where she stayed with a couple, Lucille and Otto Hatschek, who she came to adore. They lived near the San Francisco Bay shore. Lucille was a childhood friend of her mother.

Years later, I believe in 1995, Sheri and I visited Mill Valley and met the man she had hung out with while living at

Lucille's. I remember Sheri's enthusiasm as we searched for the house she had stayed in 30 years earlier and found the right family. At the time, I had no idea who greeted us when we arrived but they knew her and Otto and Lucille. I later found out that Lucille had passed away in 1978 and Otto in the middle of the 1980s.

Sheri showed me around the area, to the places she had hung out. We even found an old bridge over the estuary to an island where she hung out when she needed quiet. Her stay made a huge impression on her.

These summers meant so much to her because in Lucille and Otto, she saw a glimpse of what a true family could be like. They both accepted her as a friend with no pressure. She relaxed for the first time in her life and enjoyed what she considered to be freedom. This summer made a profound impact on her. She still talked about how much Lucille did for her even 30 and 40 years later.

After her graduation in December 1970 with a degree in psychology, she returned home to Arizona.

After her return home, in early to mid-1971, she became pregnant and decided not to have the child. I don't know the date for sure since she only mentioned this to me a few times. She also had a great dislike for children and never wanted to have any. A few years later she had a hysterectomy.

Her grandmother, Winifred Rehme, passed away January 21, 1972, three years after the 50th wedding anniversary. In June 1972, she enrolled in the University of Arizona at Tucson, where she pursued her master's degree in alcoholism rehabilitation. She completed the degree September 28, 1973 with her thesis, *Evaluation of Prescheduled Relapses in Chronic Alcoholics.*

Sheri and dog Sam in New Jersey house

In anticipation of graduation, she moved to Princeton, New Jersey, where she took a job at the Princeton House Alcoholism Program as an alcoholism counselor. In a Princeton House flyer dated August 13, 1973, it's noted she also provides information and transportation to Alcoholics Anonymous meetings.

While in college, she had met Jay Easley, a photographer, and married him December 31, 1973. She lived with him in Princeton, New Jersey. She told me about six months into the marriage, in July 1974, he struck her and she gathered up her belongings and her dog Sam and drove cross country back to Yuma, where her divorce from him became final July 1, 1975 in Yuma County Superior Court.

After three attempts to escape life in Yuma, in the summer of 1974, she found herself right back where she had started, in Yuma. I don't know if she had an apartment or lived with her parents. Sheri did leave two newspaper clippings from late 1974, one for an alcoholism treatment course at Kofa High

School starting September 11, 1974 and another for a panel discussion on "Drugs, Alcohol, and Venereal Disease" at the Arizona State Nurses Association meeting November 24, 1974, where she moderated the meeting as a social worker. In 1975, she moved back to Tucson and made her final escape from home.

Why This Section is Important

This chapter became even more difficult to write as I discovered new material about her first few years. I lived with her for 23 years and heard only a few snippets of how she felt about these years. I knew they were difficult but did not understand how difficult. I think it is a wonder she survived as well as she did.

Her first 20 years set the stage for her last nine days. To understand what happened in the

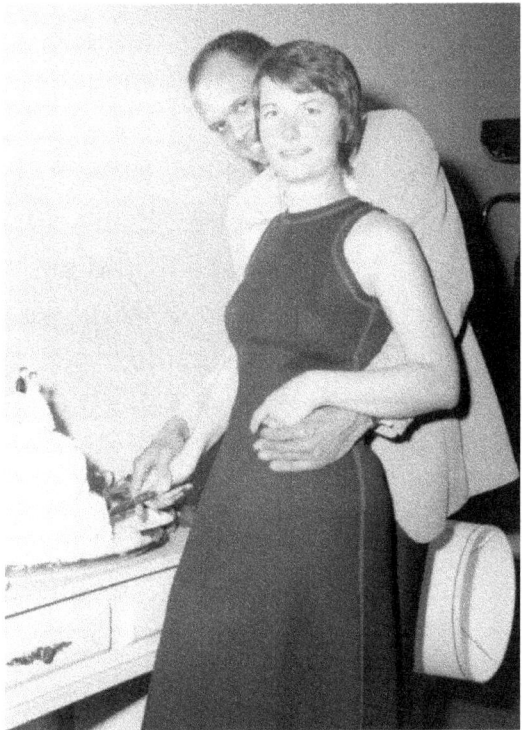

Sheri and Jay on wedding day

end, you must understand what happened at the start. It amazes me how much of our belief systems, personal self-confidence, and sense of self-worth are set by the time we start school and how, as in Sheri's case, most of our school years are spent in a fight to survive our first few years.

This is important because most people who knew Sheri in her later years saw her as a fun-loving professional who loved to make friends and help people live better. Only a few close friends knew about the dark underpinnings, the lack of confidence, the life-long need for a family that cared, the businesses and work that went so far and no farther.

Whether we are parents with children or the product of a disastrous childhood, we must understand how our random actions (or at times deliberate actions), our habits, our ways of discipline, our random comments, can affect whole lives. Even Sheri, a therapist and consultant most of her life, could not get past it.

I remember the shock when I read the order Sheri's mother gave her at the age of 4: "Don't call me Mommy." Sheri had to ask for her name so she would know what to call her.

Even sixty years later, thirty years after her mother's death, she called her mother Willa.

As adults, we must believe in our value before others will believe in us. It is easy to get frozen in the attitudes of our youth.

In the next section, you will meet the young woman who emerged from this terrifying childhood and better understand of how she coped, or didn't cope, with her past.

Part II

2015

Monday,

The Second Day in November

ONE

Everything Changes,
Part 1,
Monday, November 2, 2015

If Monday begins to sound a bit like Sunday, it's by design. We dedicated the first few routine days of this journey to Sheri's comfort and, as we all know, physical comfort is important in the last stages of life. However, changes began in these days which led to the extraordinary events later in the week. The main players moved into and out of the picture as they set the stage for Act I.

I knew Susan planned to get up about 3:30 a.m. so Alice could sleep before the new day began. Susan, one of Sheri's best friends from the corporate world, was her business partner for a few months in 1999. I knew she wanted to spend every possible minute here to help take care of Sheri. When I got up about 8 a.m., it surprised me to find Alice up and Susan gone.

Alice looked exhausted and depressed.

"What happened?" I asked.

She told me Susan had received a phone call about 5 a.m. Her husband Barry, in Hospice in San Diego for several months, took a sudden turn for the worse and she needed to be with him.

"I don't know what to do," Alice said. "All of Sheri's friends are exhausted and now we don't have Susan. Her medications are more complicated and Sheri can't participate in her care."

I looked at the schedule for the next few nights. We had penciled Susan in for at least two more nights later in the week, a big hole to fill.

"What can we do?" I asked.

Alice said she had read through the Hospice book the night before. "I discovered they have three levels of care, the current one, respite care to allow the caretaker out of the house, and 24-hour nursing care. I'll ask our Hospice RN if we can get a higher level of care."

I had no idea how we would manage the next few days. This is one of the frustrating parts of caregiving. So much is expected and neither Alice nor I had professional expertise at medical care. We guessed half the time and called for support the other half. We didn't know the standards of care for a person in Sheri's situation. With several different people on the overnight schedule, we already had problems and often guessed at the best solutions. We decided to wait for Hospice RN to arrive.

The RN had read the weekend reports but had not seen Sheri since Friday. The dramatic change in Sheri's condition since then surprised her.

She and Alice and I had a lengthy conversation about the medications, the problems with her morphine and Ativan and all the confusion about how to handle emergencies as they arose. Alice asked her if Hospice could do more for us.

She checked Sheri for a few minutes, then turned and said, "We start 24-hour nursing care right now. The first nurse will arrive at 4 p.m. I'll order a morphine pump so she gets a steady dose of the medication."

We talked further about how to handle the situation until the first nurse arrived. I asked her how much longer before Sheri passed.

"When did she eat last?" she asked.

She hadn't eaten for at least three or four days, the last nutrition being a bit of miso soup and rice and mango lasse juice Saturday.

"From her condition and what I know about how it can go from this point, I would guess she has 12 hours to a day at most," she said.

This surprised me but also evoked a sense of relief that Sheri might at last find peace. She endured so much pain and discomfort over the previous few days and declared she did not want to linger more than necessary. She told us she wanted to go twice before she went into a deep sleep. I also remembered a comment from Alice. After Sheri awakened the day before, she asked, "Why am I still here?"

Every day she lay on the bed unable to speak for herself hurt all of us.

Twenty-four-hour nursing care lifted the burden of uncertainty. Now we knew Sheri would get professional care, not the amateur efforts we provided. We could let go of care for her physical body and concentrate on her spiritual needs. We could talk to her spirit and leave the physical to the nurses.

Alice and I both relaxed and cancelled the list of people who volunteered to stay overnight to care for Sheri. Alice said she would stay the night with no problem. We couldn't wait for the first nurse to arrive.

About 10:45 a.m. Pedro and Sabina, our housekeepers, arrived. I had forgotten about them in all the confusion. They had worked for us for years both in Laguna Woods and at our house in Irvine and become good friends. They hadn't seen Sheri for two weeks so I had to explain her condition to them. What a sad moment!

I went out for lunch while Alice watched Sheri. After I got back, the Hospice aide who bathed patients, arrived. Sheri still wore the same green dress she had worn since late the previous week and the aide found it difficult to move her to remove the dress. She had to cut it off. We found an old t-shirt of mine to cover her while she gave Sheri her last bath.

Routine dominated the rest of the afternoon. Another good friend, Sherree Jolly, arrived ready to spend the night. The morphine pump arrived at four and the Hospice RN arrived a few minutes later to install it. The pump ran from a line the nurse inserted under the skin for maximum comfort and delivered a continuous flow of five milliliters of medication per hour. In addition, if she had pain, we could press a button every 15 minutes to deliver an additional dose. She also ordered liquid Ativan for anxiety.

The first hint of trouble came at 4:30 p.m., when the first Hospice LVN arrived, half an hour late. In our moment of relief, we turned the medications over to her and relaxed. I went out and got a hamburger for dinner and bought ice cream for Alice and Sherree. I got home at 7.

Alice told me the nurse had wanted to rearrange all the medications and support supplies. Sheri showed great discomfort so they pushed the medication button several times.

By the time the first nurse left, we had an extensive list of protocols to discuss with the RN the next morning. She had written the medical orders the wrong way and the nurses refused to make changes. The first Hospice LVN left about 11 p.m. and the second one arrived late again, about 11:30 after a 20-minute delay at the gate.

At least Sheri rested better even if the nursing situation did not match our expectations.

Sherree and Alice spent the night with her.

Divine order always flows perfectly. Part of the grand order. I flow easily and effortlessly. I get all my projects completed perfectly with ease and competence. I let go of doubt because the truth I'm always working with God's love. God's Love cradles me and energizes me. I am sooo grateful for this wonderful knowing and confident feeling. I let go and flow.
Sheri Long
October 24, 2012

TWO

Everything Changes,
Part 2,
May and June 2014

I like to call these two months the lull before the storm. Sheri continued her recovery from surgery through the last week of May and by June went back to work on a limited basis.

We both believed removal of the pheo, the critter, as she called it, fixed the problem. Her recovery passed without incident. The tiny incisions healed and the pain in her back faded to a weak echo of her previous pain, or so we wanted to believe.

We saw Dr. Granlund on June 10, a routine visit. We had no other medical attention. Sheri felt so well we went to Frontier Trainings in San Diego June 16 to 25 and took three courses.

Her recovery from surgery continued and she could not participate fully. She even took a sleeping bag into the training room in case she needed to take a nap. Clinton Swaine, wonderful as always, gave her all the support she needed.

In San Diego, we stayed at Susan Leone's house despite the mess as she packed it up before she rented it out. The big advantage for us? Fifteen minutes from the training room and the perfect rent: free! The boxes piled high in every room didn't matter. Sheri even made it worse when she let a mouse into the house through the back door.

Sheri still lacked energy so she stayed home the first day of the training. A month after the surgery, she still had pain in her back. Although she recovered well from the adrenal surgery, she still lacked her normal energy.

Her recovery felt normal. After all, it takes time to recover from major surgery. We had no reason to believe a problem existed. As the days passed in the training room, she went from a lot of time at rest in the back of the room to a lot of time in active participation. She improved but not as much as I wanted to see. After we got home, Sheri mentioned low energy from time to time. We became more concerned since the back pain had not subsided as we expected.

Still, I remember our optimism that we would find an answer.

Before the month ended, Sheri heard Laguna Laughter Yoga would hold its usual Fourth of July fireworks party off Main Beach in Laguna. This highlight of the year event happened at an apartment near the beach no more than a few hundred yards from where the fireworks rocketed into the sky. An amazing spectacle! We looked forward to it with great anticipation.

THREE

World Travelers, July 1996 to August 2000

1997 Trip to Mexico

I'll give you a lot of detail in this section because it shows the depth of Sheri's pain over the trauma she suffered in her early years with a dysfunctional family she believed had let her down in so many ways. When she went to college in Mexico in the late sixties, her new adopted family gave her what her biological family never did, acceptance and love. They gave her a stake in their family and remained close for her entire life.

As her blood relatives died off one by one, the only constants in her life became her friends here and her other family in Mexico.

In May 1997, we decided to travel to Mexico to visit with the family of Sheri's godson, Paco Cabrera, in Puebla. This would be an adventure for me since I had never traveled farther south than Ensenada. I looked forward to this chance to meet this marvelous family. For her it would be a long overdue reunion.

I anticipated this trip with mixed emotions since Sheri spoke fluent Spanish and I spoke very little despite a semester course in Spanish at our local community college. Sheri did not want to become my translator every time I talked. I did learn enough Spanish to get along but not enough for complicated discussions.

We landed in Mexico City and checked into the Hotel Cortes in downtown. Then Sheri contacted a family she had known when she lived in Mexico years before. We had a great dinner with them then stayed overnight at our hotel. The next morning, we took the bus to Puebla, a two-hour ride to the east across the mountains.

I experienced Mexico through Sheri's eyes. She knew it as well as a native and spoke Spanish like a native. Many times, I heard her switch from English to Spanish and back in an instant without thought or slowdown.

We had quite an agenda in Mexico: meet the family, drive to Chiapas and the Mayan ruins at Palenque in our rental car and get better acquainted with Paco and his family.

To meet the family in Mexico involves more than you might think. We didn't sit round and chat. They treated us to a full-on barbeque with dozens of family members, Paco's aunts and uncles and cousins, his grandfather, and other family friends. I could see how much they loved Sheri by the warm greeting and the festival atmosphere of the party. The women spent hours on the tamales, the food and drink flowed, and the fun went on for hours. I tested out my Spanish and to my amazement it worked, at least a bit. The family included two medical doctors, who later took us on a tour of their clinic, and other professionals or business owners. Paco raised and trained show dogs and owned half of a veterinary clinic.

We had a fun time getting acquainted and took excursions to Cholula and Puebla. Then the time came to pick up our rental car and begin our road adventure to Southern Mexico. Rocio joined us as a guide and companion.

In Mexico, you make plans and then life happens.

We called the rental agency which had our reservation. They said they didn't have a reservation. They didn't even have a car. We are ready to go with no way to go. A quick conference with Rocio led to a conference with her husband and after a back-and-forth discussion, we reached an agreement. We would drive his car on our trip. As chance would have it, his new car had a perfect finish and we might need to drive on bad roads. We would have to be careful.

The first leg of the journey took us to Oaxaca, home to the wonderful pre-Aztec ruins of Monte Alban and to the villages where most of the carved and painted animals we see here in the United States are made. Paco followed us with his wife and children as we drove on a sunny hot day through a dry desert. About halfway to Oaxaca, Paco pulled over the side of the freeway and stopped, jumped out and searched all around his car.

"Something blew up," he said. He opened the hood and looked at the engine. Normal. No smoke. No water sprays. No drips.

He looked at the tires. Normal.

He walked around the car several times. No problems.

Then he opened the trunk. At first it looked normal but then we noticed dampness in one corner. Paco reached in, rummaged around, and pulled out a ruptured soft drink can.

He smiled. The can sat right next to the wheel well. The spin of the tire heated the well until the can swelled up and burst under the pressure.

We all had a good laugh (a relieved laugh), jumped back in our cars and headed south.

We had two objectives in Oaxaca, eat, stay overnight, see ruins, and buy stuff. The last meant the most to Sheri. Clothing stalls, jewelry stores, whatever, she spent hours shopping.

Before we left home, she knew she wanted to buy a large painted animal sculpture in Oaxaca. Many small ones are available here with high price tags but few large ones came north and those carry an astronomical price tag. Sheri could get a far better deal in Mexico.

The sculptures are hand carved from one piece of wood, and hand painted with tiny colored dots. They range from tiny, less than an inch long, to two or three feet across or more. Sheri loved lizards so the many carved lizards delighted her. We drove around Monte Alban to the villages on the other side of the mound, where dozens of carvers and painters made carved animals.

After much discussion and much haggling, we purchased a large blue and white lizard. We shipped it home in a washing machine box. Then we went to another studio, where we watched a man paint smaller green lizards. Sheri wanted one. The negotiations began. At first the man said he couldn't sell it because these were part of a large order. He continued to paint. Sheri made an offer. He painted. Paco stood around. We went in and out for about two hours. At last we made a deal and the green lizard belonged to us.

The next morning, Paco and family returned home, we had breakfast, and headed for Tehuantepec, several hundred miles to the south over a windy two-lane road.

But first.

Sheri exploring the ruins at Mitla

We had to finish breakfast. We had to see the ruins at Mitla, south of Oaxaca. We had to buy more stuff. All of which takes time. Because we took so much time at the ruins, we also had to eat lunch.

Then as we drove out of town, Sheri and Rocio spotted an outdoor market, a bunch of booths set up on a dirt lot with clothes for sale, many of them of Guatemalan origin. We had to stop and shop. Three hours later, near four o'clock in the afternoon, they announced, "We're finished," and we started south.

In Mexico, one law of the road rules. Do Not Drive After Dark on country roads. Reason? No lights line the roads. Many cars and trucks drive without headlights. Wild animals and domesticated animals roam about. You must pass trucks. You must trust the driver ahead of you. When you can move, you need to move fast.

Since I had never driven in Mexico after dark, the late start concerned me. Sure enough, the sun went down about two hours before we arrived in Tehuantepec. I sped along, passed truck after truck, and missed all the wildlife. Rocio said I drove like a Mexican, a huge compliment. We arrived in town exhausted and way after dark. We looked forward to our room, a late dinner, and a good night's sleep.

Tehuantepec, Chiapas, and Tabasco

Way past dark and way past dinner, the lights of Tehuantepec began to glow on the horizon, a small glow to be sure, the city has about 50,000 people, but a welcome one. We would be safe from this long night drive through the southern Mexican wilderness with nary a town in sight.

As we approached the town, we noticed a lot of traffic on the bridge over a very wide river (dry) on the edge of town. This looked odd since traffic should have dissipated this long after dark. A lot of people milled about on the hillside so Sheri opened the car window and called to a young man nearby.

"What's happening," she asked in Spanish.

"We're in the middle of a taxi strike," the man said. "Nobody can get into town. The main road is blocked."

The three of us looked at each other. We knew of no other way into town.

"How do we get around it?" Sheri asked.

The young man answered as he pointed back the way we had come, then said, "It's too complicated. I need to show you."

Sheri nodded to Rocio. "Should we let him in the car?"

Rocio nodded yes.

"Okay," Sheri said. "Get in and show us where to go."

First, we turned around and drove back off the bridge and after a short distance turned into a neighborhood. A dirt road led toward the river.

"Keep on," the man said.

I drove down the road, then noticed it ended. He pointed straight ahead. "Keep on." The road ended. We drove through brush, then across the dry part of the river. I noticed a stream of headlights in front of us in the riverbed and realized how inventive a solution the townspeople had come up with for the taxi strike. We followed a back road into the riverbed, drove down the dry river, under the bridge, and up an embankment on the other side. Dozens of people on the riverbank guided drivers up the steep bank and into town. As we arrived, we all thanked our guide and headed for our hotel.

Tehuantepec had only two hotels. We had reserved a $10 per night room. Now we knew Mexican hotels and had no illusions we would sleep in a Hilton or even Motel 6. The room had a door, windows, no air conditioning, two beds, and a bathroom, the shower and toilet next to each other in the same room.

We also discovered a roommate, a large black cockroach hanging out on the wall. Sheri, an old desert hand, liked bugs so she welcomed the big guy and we took a couple of photos of him.

By now you get a good picture of how Sheri traveled: adventure by adventure. The weirder the events the better. No fancy hotels for us. True, most of time we stayed in decent local establishments at a higher cost, but none this bad. At times, as you saw earlier, we stayed with families.

After we checked in and got settled, we walked the block or so to the central square to get dinner. Sheri found a mango stand and bought one. She forgot to wash it and ended up with intestinal problems for a few days.

By now you get the idea. The rest of the trip brought us adventures we don't need to go into detail on. The next day we drove to San Cristobal de las Casas, a beautiful town in a valley surrounded by mountains in Chiapas with cool days and clear skies. We hung out for several days, attended Easter festivities, visited nearby Indian towns and a Maya Catholic Church. We dined well and had a wonderful time.

The rest of the trip included a drive downhill into sticky heat to the Maya ruin at Palenque, then to Villahermosa, where the heat forced us out of town as soon as possible. Then we hit the Isle of the Monkeys (fascinating place filled with very fat and well-fed monkeys), then back to Puebla.

I think this taste for adventure reflected a childhood with little adventure and much danger. When we went into small communities and met the locals, they accepted us as family and welcomed us in. She didn't care for museums although she put up with my desire to visit them. She wanted to meet people, see the culture, and enjoy unusual ways to think and act. I never once saw her judge anyone for their cultural differences. She immersed herself and became part of the culture, like a native, not a visitor. You will see a lot more of this as we go through the next few sections.

Manchitas, the Mexican Immigrant

In the last part of 1997, Sheri mentioned she wanted a dog. I had not had one since elementary school, when we had a cute mongrel named Butch in the back yard. I didn't want a dog since we already had cats but Sheri kept up talk about the wonderful dogs she had as a child so the discussion continued but no action ensued.

As an aside, the dogs she had were the one part of her home life she liked. The memory must have stuck as she had several dogs in her Tucson and Hemet days. The dog in many ways gave her the comfort she needed to feel safe.

The next summer, her godson's family invited us to return to Mexico because Paco had opened a new veterinary clinic with a friend and he also wanted to show us around the area. We caught a plane and headed south again.

As soon as we arrived, dogs surrounded us. They barked all day and barked all night. At the vet clinic, in one back room we saw a dozen cages, each with a dog inside. Sheri noticed this cute puppy, white with rust-colored markings. The next day she walked the pup with Paco and his other dogs. This curious, active, and healthy if a bit flea-bitten dog captured her heart.

Paco raised show dogs and entered them in local and regional contests. He had several champions and many excellent placers.

One day, Sheri asked where the pup she liked had come from. Paco said they had left the door open a few minutes too long one night before he locked up. When they arrived the next morning, they found the pup inside and nobody had the heart to throw her out.

She asked Paco's wife, "What will you do with the dog?"

"She's not a show dog. We will put her to sleep."

"No, you won't," Sheri said. "We'll take her home." She turned to me. "Won't we!" I nodded. What else could I do?

Attention turned to how this might be done. It is not easy to transfer dogs from one country to another. We found it might be harder to take the dog out of Mexico than to get her into the United States. We needed a veterinarian to certify she had all her shots and Paco had one on staff. Sheri, as the new owner of the dog, gave her a flea bath (we have photos) and a new name, Manchitas. Manchas in Spanish are spots so the name meant little spots. At the time Manchitas fit into two hands like a tiny ball of fur. We had no idea she would grow up to be a 40-pound adult dog.

We did the usual visitor stuff for a week or so then prepared to leave. We got the certificate, had the Mexican vet at the airport certify her worthy to depart and got on the plane with Manchitas in a carry box in the passenger cabin.

All went well until we arrived in Dallas, Texas. Well, attempted to arrive. A huge thunderstorm attacked the city and after two passes, the pilot announced we would head to Austin to wait out the storm for two or three hours.

When we landed in Austin, the government considered the plane to still be in Mexico since we had not yet cleared customs and immigration, which meant nobody got off, including dogs who might need to pee. As we sat in Austin, people on the plane got to know Manchitas. The stewardesses got her water and set out towels in case she needed them.

By the time we headed back to Dallas we had already missed our connecting flight to Orange County and might miss the next one, a nine o'clock flight scheduled to land a few minutes before the Orange County Airport closed.

Of course, the storm had made a mess of air traffic in Dallas. First, we had to get the little dog into the country. The immigration officer asked for her papers, glanced at them and let her pass. We got on the last plane out and waited. Massive numbers of planes waited in line to take off before us.

We got out of the gate, waited, got in line, and after a long wait, took off. The pilot assured us he would work to get us to Orange County on time. You already know what happened next. The plane had to move around big clouds and by the time we got up to speed, the pilot announced we would divert to Los Angeles because Orange County would not stay open for us. They would arrive about midnight, put us on the bus and drive us to Orange County Airport, where we could catch a taxi for home.

Sheri, Lee and Manchitas c 2000

We arrived home about 2 a.m., complete with dog we had no idea how to handle, no bed for her, no food for her, no way to control her, and no help in sight.

Manchitas grew up to be a bundle of energy, a sweet dog who loved to take long walks and hang out with the cats. She gave us 14 years of pleasure and passed away a few months after we moved to Laguna Woods.

Julia from Russia

Late in 1998, Sheri heard a group of students from Vladivostok, Russia needed homes to stay in while they attended a special two-week program. As you can imagine by now, Sheri wanted to join in any cultural event she could find and what could be more fun than Russia.

She volunteered to host one of the students and to our surprise we ended up as hosts to one of the leaders of the Russian team, a young woman named Julia Pisarevskaya. She and her husband and his family ran the Russian school which sent the team here.

We did get to meet many of her students but I can't overrate the value of our connection with her. She spoke good English so we could communicate. We learned about eastern Russia and Julia even gave us a large history book on Vladivostok with photos of the city and environs.

When they returned to Russia we knew we expected to never see her or any of these students again.

The end of REACH

For years, Sheri worked at comfortable job at REACH, an employee assistance company, even though it had changed hands a couple of times in the past few years. I remember the pride she took when she worked with major companies to help their executives better understand their Hispanic employees.

Since she spoke fluent Spanish, she counseled many Hispanic employees at companies like Kwikset and Nabisco.

In mid-1998, Blue Shield, a huge healthcare insurance company, purchased REACH's parent company. REACH, a tiny operation, did not register on their radar screen. Within a few months it became clear they planned to close REACH.

This became a watershed moment for Sheri. She had worked for them since 1985, a steady job with a steady paycheck. We had talked a few times about a private practice as a marriage and family counselor or a new business, her own EAP. She talked about it with her friend Susan Leone and they decided in December to see if they could buy REACH from Blue Shield for a minimal amount.

After a few days of negotiations, it looked like we owned an EAP company. She even set up a corporation with Susan, Solutions @ Work, Inc., to run it. Both Sheri and Susan celebrated until another offer showed up. Then the deal fell apart and one of the other employees at REACH ended up the new owner.

At first this blow stunned both Susan and Sheri. Their new company commenced business January 1, 1999 with no clients or prospect of clients. Sheri had no work with no prospects for the near future.

I remember the next few months as filled with a frenzy of activity and discussion over the future destination of the company. At first, they decided to start their own EAP company and see how many companies they could sign up. This meant policies and procedures, rate schedules, perhaps new hires. After a few months, I knew Sheri had little interest in EAP as a full-time project although she indicated she would take on EAP jobs from other providers if asked, which she did for the next 10 years, as it turned out.

By August 1999, it became clear she and Susan did not agree on the future of the company. They agreed to split up. Sheri bought Susan's half of the company for an agreed upon amount and they parted friends.

We know business partnerships can destroy friendships. So many times, we hear of people who never speak again to one another after a business venture falls apart.

Sheri did not let that happen to her. She and Susan made sure their years-long friendship stayed intact. For Sheri, her friends meant more to her than business disagreements. When it became evident the partnership would not work out, they did what so many people don't, they talked about it.

Sheri's attitude is a perfect example of how to do this right, so everyone walks away happy. She now owned her own corporation and clients, and a new burst of happiness and exhilaration. And she still had one of her best friends.

We go to Russia!

I could write all day about this adventure. It happened because Sheri took many wild ideas seriously. I don't suppose most of us would want to end up in the hinterlands of Russia, where very few tourists ever go. However, Sheri wanted to meet people, not see sites and as it turned out, the deal came with free airfare, lodging, and food.

In late 1999, again the same time she opened her new business, she heard a program called Citizens Democracy Corps, funded in part by USAID, sent teams of professional experts to countries who needed expert trainers. Among the places on the list: Macedonia, Kosovo, Burma, Romania, and Russia.

Sheri came home one day and said, "I heard about this great program where you can go to Russia as volunteer consultants." I had no idea what to think. Maybe a passing fantasy? I knew she made passing fantasies into reality.

She contacted the program and told them, "I don't have much business experience, and own a small company here in California I started last year."

The program manager said, "No problem. In Russia, they don't know how to run companies or market or sell. Because you live in the United States, you know far more than they do and have a lot to teach them."

Soon the fantasy became an offer, and then an assignment, a leather tanning factory in Rostov-on-Don in southern Russia.

Then she asked them if I could get an assignment too. She told them about my newspaper and magazine management experience and they assigned me to work with two newspapers in Rostov.

They even set dates, July 2000, and paid all our expenses.

We didn't need a lot of preparation. Sheri read up on the Russian leather tanning business but, since we had no knowledge of the company's situation, we couldn't go further.

We also set up a couple of Servas visits (like the French experience) in Moscow because we could, one with a psychologist near the center of the city and the other with a retired couple in southern Moscow.

When we arrived, our host in Moscow first took us to an American Diner and then signed us into the Hotel Rossiya, a Brezhnev era monstrosity of a hotel so bad the Russians tore it down a few years later. It had two entrances and stretched a quarter of a mile long. We reached our first room, on the tenth floor about as far as we could get from the desk, after a trek of about 15 minutes. The furniture dated from at least the 1980s.

The first Servas visit landed us in an apartment so filthy we abandoned it after one night. Imagine garbage overflowing from the kitchen trash can into the living room. On the other hand, don't imagine it. We went back to the Rossiya for a night, then on to our second hosts.

Such a contrast. The couple, a retired geologist and retired botanist, lived on a $24 per month pension. For breakfast, they served us tomatoes and potatoes. Lunch? The same. Dinner? The same.

Despite the lack of money, they lived in a clean, homey apartment with a tiny bathroom that only served up cold water.

Sheri and Lee with our Russian hostess in Moscow

They escorted us to a nearby priory and then to the Novodevichy Cemetery, where you can find the graves of Nikita Khrushchev and a whole panoply of Communist notables such as Stalin's first wife and Molotov and Malenkov, among others. Stupendous monuments stood along tree-lined pathways of the most fascinating cemetery I have ever visited. One grave even featured a monster statue of a man on the telephone.

Then we went to Rostov to do our consulting gig. The highlights included wonderful Russian hosts, a boat trip on the Don River, a drive to Taganrog, the birthplace of Checkhov, and a drive to Novocherkassk, an old Cossack City surrounded by rivers and fields.

We also lived in a Russian apartment and went to work each day with a Russian driver.

As the true highlight of the Rostov weeks, we took a quick flight to Istanbul, Turkey, where the high energy reminded us of the stark contrast with Russia, with its deserted streets. We even attended a Turkish festival where Sheri invited herself onto the stage when they announced a belly dance contest and ran away with the top prize when she exhibited the results of years of belly dance classes.

We stayed an additional week in Moscow, where we found Julia and her husband and got a great tour of the area. By then he worked for the Duma and she had a young child.

We flew home exhausted but ecstatic, ready for new adventures.

FOUR

Starting Out,
1975-1980

This is one of the strangest periods in Sheri's life for me because she talked about it less than any other.

I've paged through photo albums and envelopes of pictures looking for a better handle on what happened and what it meant. I see a lot of incidents: another move to Tucson, a bit more time in Yuma, then a sudden move to Hemet, California in 1980. I see a trip or two to Mexico she may have participated in and several shadowy boyfriends who rated a packet or two of photos each.

Over these years, she escaped the day to day presence of her parents but not the effect. She often mentioned she spent decades in therapy but never gave dates. She had a love-hate relationship with Bill and Willa for many years after the two of them separated. She wanted their approval and could never get it. She loved the idea of great parents and hated the reality of the self-centered father and mother she saw instead. Her father stopped drinking in the early 70's but her mother never did. Bill had his business and his new wives. Willa had her unhappy life at home on the ranch in Yuma.

Sheri did talk a lot about 1983 and 1984 as watershed years, when both Bill and Willa passed away, she of a stroke and he of a heart attack. "My world ended, my family vanished," she told me in the early 90s, soon after we met. "My history was gone, my connection to the past was severed. My life was never the same."

I saw this strong connection to her past as based not on her actual past but the past she wished she had lived. While the past actors still lived, they could change and give her the validation she needed. With them gone, she had no hope.

Now you know why it is so hard to get a good grip on these years. Her attitude verged on backward looks even as she worked to build a career, give speeches, and look forward to her new life. She pushed forward with determination, her past in tow, a drag every step.

I think her failed marriage may have played a part in this process. She did meet other men, even lived with them, even connected with them. However, she never committed to any of the relationships so they petered out like a faded sunset.

This is an odd moment to write this chapter. It is the day after Valentine's Day, 2016, the second anniversary of the visit to the emergency room where her final illness began. I thought yesterday might be more emotional than it turned out to be. My bad cough and lack of energy may well may have made a difference.

As I think about it now, the months we spent in search of the cause of her illness parallel her search for an answer to the contradictions in her family life. In 2014, Sheri made it a task to find out why she had back pains, with a very strong certainty it would turn out well, even as the prospects continued to turn darker and more foreboding.

She wanted the happy family she had never known and she

Sheri in Mexico 1975

wanted the healthy body she enjoyed to last into the future. Her family faded away in much the same way her healthy body turned on her with a vengeance she never understood. She accepted she might die but never understood why this event could happen to her.

Her end became one more betrayal. Ironic.

Why This Chapter Is So Difficult

I wrote the above section four months ago and although a lot has happened since then, I made little headway on this chapter. It had promise yet not much happened. Anyway, as I write this it is June 4, 2016, the first real Spring day in a while. I am in Laguna Beach to savor a lemon and mint chocolate gelato at our favorite place, Dolce Gelato on Broadway. Sheri and I shared many a gelato here with friends and with ourselves at times. I don't have a pad of paper, so I write this on a napkin. After a hot day, by the time I got to Laguna, a deep gray marine layer blocked the sunset and the gray waves rose as the twilight deepened. With the ocean at high tide, the beaches vanished beneath waves that crashed on the shoreline rocks. It felt like a winter storm in Spring.

What a weird few months. I stayed away from Laguna after January. I felt in between, not ready to do much but bored. The Writers Workshop is ready to sell, I speak more and have finished a client's book project.

I took a while to write this chapter because I had a difficult time with the events of the late 70s. A few days ago, I found another book of notes by Sheri about her life in this period. In her own mixed-up words, written February 2, 1990, she said:

"Age 25-32, Fast track, a blur, dated, lots of jobs, moved to Tucson, Arizona, moved around. Lots of motion, running??? Thought having a good time – what's a good time??? Fun? With guys. Divorce at 26, drove across country, created jobs, kept moving. School-great feeling, being good at school. Focused on external satisfaction?? No goals, not self-destructive, get by, existing, no fear?? Of commitments? In Germany cried, fearful, could not communicate, out of gas. Disco, fast, aggressive behavior. Punching. Why?? Beneficial?? Bored with the lifestyle, looking for something. Where was what I was looking for?? Decade birthday party fun, lots of dates. Superficial striving, searching, no major achievements, moving fast so I didn't feel. Lots/bits – little commitment. Fear of commitment. Moved on to Tucson, unemployed, migraine, and psychocomatic."

The drift she talks about is like the feelings I had over the last few months. My research came to her time of uncertainty at the same time I arrived at mine. As I watched the waves I thought about how much she loved this town, the beach, and the scene. Trips down here for Laughter Yoga and to explore with friends, helped center her and I know it does the same for me.

We must go through the gloom before the good times begin. As you will see on the next few pages, a lot happened. Now that you know how she reacted to it, here are the details as far as

The Cabrera Family of Puebla

I can reconstruct them. Here we go.

Mexico and the Move back to Tucson

In January 1975, when she still lived in Yuma, Sheri traveled to Mexico to attend the wedding of one of the members of her godson Paco's extended Cabrera family. He was five at the time. As I said before, she considered this family her own and they did the same.

Paco and parents 1975

I'm sure this trip, her first time in Mexico since graduation from the University of the Americas in 1970, meant a lot to her. It looked from the photos like a festive visit. She took a lot of photos and collected postcards to commemorate the trip. After time with the family, she visited Mexico City, the Mitla ruins near Oaxaca, and several locations around Merida, Yucatan.

As I looked at the 40-year-old photo of the extended family, I recognized a few of them from our visit in 1997. She loved the Cabreras, the only real extended family she had. They treated her like a queen whenever she visited them.

Sheri and father Bill at Big Bear. I found other happier photos of this trip but none of the two of them together.

Anyway, back from Mexico, Sheri lives in Tucson, starts a counseling practice, lives with a new boyfriend and rebuilds her life. I found a few documents from this era but not many. In early 1980, she left Tucson and moved to Hemet with her boyfriend.

Later in the same year, Sheri and her father Bill and step-mother Jan went on a trip to Big Bear in the mountains north of Los Angeles. I know she liked to share time with him and visited him at the house in Lido Isle in Newport Beach quite often.

She had moved back to Tucson and started her new social worker practice by then. She kept two brochures from alcoholism events, one in May and one in December 1975, both in Tucson, which would indicate her presence in the area.

When we visited Tucson after we got married, she took me out to the Arizona-Sonora Desert Museum west of town. She became a docent for them in March 1977 and led tours of the facility. I enjoyed my visit to this impressive museum. I think she became a docent because she loved all kinds of desert animals like lizards, snakes and toads. We had plenty of lizards around our house in Laguna Woods and she loved to see them and play with them.

In October 1975, she and her friend Judy visited the Desert Museum and took a bunch of photos (the only ones of the

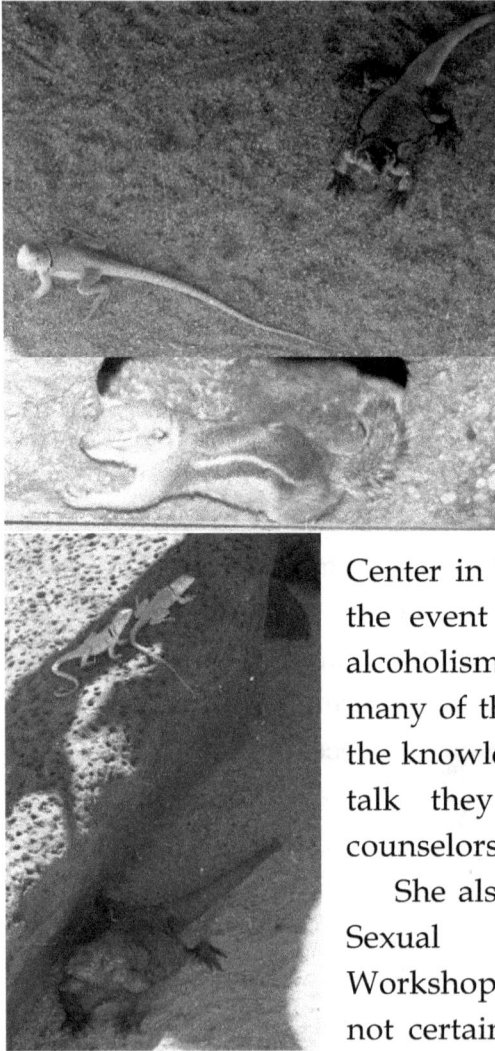

museum days I found). As I expected, she took a lot of photos of the tiny critters she so enjoyed.

Here is a sampling.

She continued to live and work in Tucson over the next three years. In March 1977, she gave a program on Sexuality and Special Populations at the Planned Parenthood Center in Tucson. The coordinator of the event wrote to her, "I am sure alcoholism has touched the lives of many of the participants and through the knowledge they gained from your talk they will be more effective counselors."

She also kept a brochure from the Sexual Attitudes Reassessment Workshop held in October 1977. I am not certain whether she presented at the event but it would make sense given she kept the brochure.

I mention these items because they show how she grew as a professional in the field of alcohol counseling and rehabilitation while she lived in Tucson.

I also found a very nice photo of Sheri and her mother taken in August 1977. I like this one because it shows a very confident and stylish young woman. I hope they both had a rare happy moment together.

The next year, 1978, turned out to be an eventful year. She often talked about her stay with a German family in Bielefeld, Germany and how she had learned enough German to communicate with them. She enjoyed close involvement with the culture of every country she visited. For instance, when we went to France in 1996, we studied French for a year and stayed with French families. Sheri's mother wrote her a very excited letter June 23, 1978 about the German trip and other family items and since it is the only letter of Willa's I found, here it is in full:

Hi, kid,

I am really terribly sorry to disappoint you but I have looked everywhere I can think of and cannot find a snapshot of you when you were little. All I have are the portraits and can't send those. Guess I'll never find them, unless I move. A bunch of them were accidentally destroyed where they were stored – but I do have a precious few somewhere.

I am tickled that the German guys called you. Was hoping the family would be fun for you. Do they speak English? Have they done this before? I envy you. It would be a fantastic experience and one I would have loved. Still would. Would be great if they could visit you later.

Your dog is bugging me. I fed him and he wouldn't leave me alone. Those allergy pills are making him gain weight – but he doesn't care – still thinks ought to eat like a horse. The pills make the open sores disappear – so he has to take them. Fat or no fat.

Went to Phx (Phoenix) Friday to doctor. Have lost 4 pounds in last three months. 96 lbs. He is finally getting concerned! Gave me Rx for appetite builder. Supposed to call me today with test results - but hasn't, after I hurried home especially to be here.

Called Dad – his spider bite symptoms have disappeared and he's feeling pretty good. After me to come visit. Summer is such a terrible time to go there. Guess I'll work it in somehow.

Pam called Friday or Saturday. They've moved in their new house. Want me to come over next weekend. Maybe I will. Would rather go to San Diego where it's cool. Their house has swamp cooler. Doesn't sound too great for 104-degree weather.

I'm so carried away with this well water you wouldn't believe it. Can't quit talking about it. I had to be out of my mind to put up with the other stuff for 24 years! I can water this whole yard in less than 1/2 day. The pool is clear all the time. We have all the water pressure we can handle. Laundry gets done in half the time. From now on I'm going to quit putting up with gross inconveniences.

Tell your German family hello for me. If they come to the States I would love to have them here.

Take care of yourself, luv.

Write.

Love you, Willa

To answer your? What I WOULD LIKE FROM Germany. Anything you think I would enjoy.

I like this letter for a couple of reasons. It's a good intro to the Germany trip but it also is the first indication we have of Willa's illness. She opens it with the words "Hi kid," which makes sense considering her order to Sheri to never call her Mommy. The dog she refers to is Sam, who didn't live much longer. She also signs it "Willa."

She refers to Sheri's trip in enviable terms when in less than six months, she and Harold would be in Egypt, where he worked with President Anwar Sadat on desert agriculture. Over the next few years, Harold and Willa would travel to Egypt several times as well as to Italy and Spain. Her health problems followed her on those travels, including a stroke while in Spain.

Sheri (third from right) and the other members of the Bielefeld tour group

Bielefeld, Germany

Sheri traveled to Bielefeld with a large tour group and stayed with local German families in early July 1978. This trip became one of the highlights of this period and she mentioned it quite often in general conversation and whenever she met anyone from Germany.

While in the country, they traveled to several major German cities, crossed into East Berlin a couple of times, and visited the Netherlands and Cologne.

From the photos she took, she must have had a wonderful time exploring the byways of northern Germany. It's clear she enjoyed the family she stayed with, Rudy and Martina Spalthof, By July 19 they arrived in the Netherlands and then Cologne and then Bielefeld. They all flew back to the United States July 25, 1978.

Harold and Willa Travel

Sheri looked up to her step-father Harold because he became like a real father to her after her birth father ran away from home, but also because he became a rock of stability in an otherwise damaged family. Willa never stopped drinking and Sheri mentioned a few times this made Harold uncomfortable but he never knew how to deal with it.

When Egypt's President Sadat asked him to come to Egypt to help them with desert agriculture, she now had a relative to brag about. I still have the albums of those trips. Harold and Sadat appear together twice, which is remarkable. Harold knew his business. The photos show crops and travel and more crops.

I met Harold later in his life, in his 80s. His gruff and opinionated manner contrasted with his bright mind and clear purpose in life. He never bragged about what he accomplished.

Part III

2015

Tuesday,

The Third Day in November

How do I embrace the inner child? Who is the inner child? The inner child is Annie Fanny, the little girl my mother named a long time ago. I like the little girl in me. She is lotsa fun. We play well together. When she needs reassurance, I get her in touch with nurturing folks as I'm not looking to my adult yet to do that. I'm glad I'm writing this. It's making me aware of my need to take care of Annie, instead of sucking off others' refreshing, nourishing juices. What about my own? It's not true that I've given them all away. I have plenty of nourishment for me. I'm just avoiding bringing those juices up and flourishing in them. They're there for the taking. I just need to avail myself of them. Is it a trust issue? Don't I trust myself to be able to reassure Annie? Let's get with it. No more victim crap! Godammit! Remember? That victim crap is Annie whining I used to get hit in the mouth for whining or crying. I don't need to keep beating the kid. Nurture the kid! It's OK, Annie. I'm taking care of you now. I'm competent. You can trust me. I've gotten my life in order. It's not perfect, but I'm in this program and I'm making progress. You can see I'm working hard at it, reading Women Who Love Too Much, attending group ACA, playing, working, getting $ stable, abstaining from my addiction to sugar, reading daily affirmations aloud every a.m., detaching from the alcoholic in my life and taking care of my needs.

Sheri Long
June 13, 1986

ONE

The Waiting Game, Part 1, Tuesday, November 3, 2015

Tuesday became a day of discovery but not the kind we wanted. In our relief at the new 24-hour nursing care for Sheri, we forgot we might still have to pay attention to the nurses. Turns out Sheri had pain much of the night and the nurse followed the written orders left by the lead nurse the previous day, which were very different from what needed to be done.

At 8 a.m., the morning LVN nurse arrived. After the earlier nurses, we loved to work with her. She understood the situation and did an excellent job helping Sheri get more comfortable.

When the Hospice RN, walked in about 10, she was surprised to see Sheri still alive. We discussed the problems of the previous evening with dosages and Sheri's position while she slept and she said she would get new orders from the

91

doctor. She also wrote out clear orders for the items she could handle. We also went over them with the new LVN nurse. Because of Sheri's pain, she increased the morphine drip.

In mid-afternoon, Alice got a phone call from Susan Leone. Her husband Barry had a stroke in the morning and had passed away. Susan mourned both his passing and her inability to be with Sheri.

Since Sheri was still restless, the nurse gave Sheri another dose of Ativan to calm her down. We continue to pump in additional morphine every 15 minutes. She left before noon with the situation under control so I went out for lunch and got back around three in the afternoon.

This sounds routine. We worked in "treat the body" mode as we monitored her vital signs and made sure the nurse gave her the pain and anxiety meds she needed. The nurses took care of all the details so we sat with Sheri and comforted her as best we could. She didn't eat or drink so we didn't need to worry about those items. At 4 p.m., the day LVN nurse left and night LVN nurse arrived. A bit older and fun-loving than the others, she made the evening shift a pleasure. We continued to monitor the morphine drip and do adds as necessary. Sheri still showed signs of pain even while unconscious.

For the rest of this routine evening, Sheri's condition did not change. She did not get worse or better. She maintained strong pulse and oxygen levels. It looked like the RN's prediction of her immanent passing would not come true. I sat by Sheri's bed for a while and whispered to her that she could go whenever she pleased. We could think of no reason for her to stay. As it turned out, she had other plans.

When we went to bed, we wondered what we would find the next morning.

TWO

The Waiting Game,
Part 2,
July to August 2014

Back in the Hospital

Surprise!

On July 2, six weeks to the day after her pheo surgery, Sheri woke up at 3 a.m. with knife-sharp pains in her abdomen and at 8 a.m. (when she finally told me about the pain) I drove her to the Saddleback Hospital Emergency Room, where the doctors took a CAT scan and admitted her to the hospital with what they thought might be a perforated ulcer.

She stayed six days in a great room with a fabulous panoramic view of the Saddleback Mountains. As we bemoaned missing our Laughter Yoga family fireworks show in Laguna Beach, we realized July 4 would be our third holiday in a row in the hospital. As the evening of July 4 darkened, the fireworks started to show up across the base of the Santa Ana Mountains a few miles east, at first one or two, then more, until we ended up with six fireworks shows.

The tests showed she had a plugged pocket (diverticulum) in the small intestine (duodenum) so they sent her home July 7 with a special diet and medicines.

Sheri took two weeks off from work and then rationed her energy to see clients and celebrated at Lee's birthday party July 23.

On July 22, we saw Dr. Weinberg and on the 28th we had another inconclusive CAT scan of the abdomen. After an Emergency Room visit July 30, Sheri got another ten days of antibiotics and improved. She even saw clients on July 31.

Seven days later, crazy itching woke her up. The pharmacists guessed the antibiotics caused it so the on-call doctor discontinued them.

The itching didn't go away. On August 10, the itching and black stool sent her back to the Emergency Room and they again admitted her to the hospital for blood in the stool. One test, an endoscopy, found the source of the blood but its other purpose, to find the source of the pain in her small intestine, failed when the camera ran into swelling at the start of the small intestine and couldn't move beyond.

Doctors decided they didn't know what caused her original pain and, because of the rarity of a diverticulum in this area, she might have an ulcer they said, but could not tell for sure.

They also discovered the swelling had pushed the pancreas against the bile duct so bile backed up into the liver, which caused the itching and jaundice of the skin. They put a drain attached to an external bag into the liver to drain the excess bile and sent her home August 16 with the bag and a liquid diet.

At this point, we felt a tinge of worry. The pheo, now long gone, could not be the problem. The new unknown critter lurked in the abdomen area, hidden from all the tests and scans. The doctors suspected ulcers or colitis but also started to talk about approval to have Dr. Imagawa at UC Irvine Medical Center, a world-renowned specialist in liver and pancreas diseases, look at her.

We decided to keep a detailed daily journal of Sheri's medical condition at this point. The presence of the liver drain bag brought home to us how dangerous this experience might become. Again, no idea cancer might be involved. However, on August 17 at 11 p.m., we noted a lot of blood clots in the bag, so many it became hard to drain so we headed for the emergency room. They changed the drainage bag and by 3:30 a.m. we went home.

On August 20, Sheri, fatigued, had to stop three times to catch her breath as she walked from the car to the house. Later in the night she couldn't keep food down. The morning of August 21, she had sharp pain at the bile drain insertion site and went back in the hospital to have it replaced. Result? No more blood, pure bile.

Sheri came home for another few days but had problems eating enough food, lack of energy, and continued weight loss. To take care of her became a full-time job. I had to find food she could eat and manage all the doctors. By the morning of August 27, the insurance approved insertion of a pic line (a nutritional feeding tube to deliver nutrients into the blood stream) to get nutrition into her. Later in the afternoon, the pic line went in and that evening Dr. Wong came by to tell us the insurance approved her to see Dr. Imagawa and she would be transferred to UCI within a day or two for further tests.

Friday morning, August 29 she wrote, "I feel better so I walked three laps around unit unassisted and packed bathroom supplies for the transfer. Rina came by and gave me a cold 'pink' sponge bath designed for Pic line owners to keep bugs out. They take lots of precautions with the precious Pic line. Good news is they take blood draws from Pic line so I'm no longer a practice pin cushion."

On Monday, September 1, Sheri transferred to UCI Medical Center by ambulance.

Sudden Consequences

When I look back on these two months, when the optimism of June collapsed into the frantic medical mess of July and August, I remember urgency with no hint of more than intestinal difficulties behind the situation.

As long as Sheri got back on her feet, I didn't worry about the situation. We had to get through it. Although Sheri continued to work off and on through the end of July, her income took a big hit when she had many weeks she could not see clients. It was also hard for me to plan for clients and market when I never knew when an emergency might arise so I stopped my regular clients and concentrated instead on the Writers Workshop, which took much less time and promised adequate income. This made me more available to Sheri as we moved through this phase of her illness. After July, Sheri's income stopped.

We got good news. The insurance we had changed to in January turned out to be very good and paid all the bills from Sheri's surgery in May, except for a few emergency room visits.

For most people, health insurance is like a black hole in the universe of stars. You know it exists but you cannot see it. Bills go in on one end and come out the other like magic, paid. Or not. Like a miracle all our bills got paid. Beyond the stars, an unknown entity made the decision to move money from one account to another. If nobody files a suit, the black hole does its job. If one day it throws up a crazy result, all you can do is run to avoid a direct hit. That never happened to us. The black hole sat, its unblinking eye focused on us, then it smiled and took care of us. As the drama unfolded, we got insurance statements with a balance of either zero or $65 for an emergency room visit. The bills mounted, first four figures, then five, then six figures and the insurance paid. Of over $1,000,000 billed for services over two years, we paid only a few thousand.

However, Sheri's lost income did put quite a hole in our finances. My income held up but the strain began to show as I had less time for clients and needed more time to take care of her. It looked increasingly like I would soon become a full-time caregiver. I had no idea how we might handle the finances, even with our Social Security income.

And we wondered: Would Dr. Imagawa give us the answers we strained to find for eight months?

My Higher Power

What about my H.P.? Thank God, I've got one now. S/He is only 6 years old in my life. Maybe I'm only 6 years old – in some ways for sure. I hand I over to my H.P. when I get too crazy with it. No, when I'm real crazy I eat something. I avoid sweets but I do eat on my anxiety to settle it. That's a big change! And I fit in my pants!!! WOW! A great side benefit. This is a good topic to get me focused on yakking to my H.P. when I'm crazy. That's the next step to curbing the compulsive overeating. Great! I got the answer. What does my H.P. mean to me? Salvation – not in the icky pious sense -- salvation from going nuts, being nuts, trying to control it, hanging on to slippery illusions, running the show, anxiety, feeling lost, incompetent, inadequate, unacceptable, less than, stupid, fat, different, separate, alone.

Sheri Long
July 11, 1986

THREE

The Waiting Game, Part 3, August 2000 to July 2005

Professional Coaches and Mentors

In late 2000, both Sheri and I discovered coaching. It appealed to Sheri because it took already successful people or people with professional challenges to new levels of success, the opposite of counseling, which focused on people in deep trouble.

She joined Professional Coaches and Mentors Association about this time. This organization had hundreds of members from successful corporate coaches to people who worked with small numbers of individuals.

She began to promote her business of coaching and training managers to better understand and manage their Hispanic employees. She had discovered this talent when she worked in

EAP at corporations. Because she spoke Spanish, she counseled a lot of Hispanics but she also worked with executives to help them understand their employees better. She saw enormous potential with the many Hispanic workers in Southern California.

After we got back from Russia, a friend of Sheri's told her about a woman from San Diego who conducted coaching certification classes in Irvine. We both signed up, Sheri because it fit her professional future well, I because it intrigued me.

After we finished the course and got certified, I joined PCMA as a writing coach and got my start when I helped a few of the members write their books.

In 2002 print on demand started to impact the book business. John Hall at one meeting proposed a plan for PCMA to put out a book of articles by members of the organization. I raised my hand and said I would coordinate it. A year later, at the 2004 Convention, we launched the new book and watched it become the best-selling book ever at a PCMA conference.

Sheri's business successes

Around this time, Sheri signed a contract with a state-funded organization which provided leadership training to corporations in Southern California. Through them, she led training classes for local corporations such as the office furniture maker Hon Corporation. This very successful and lucrative run of trainings lasted several years. She did many of them in Spanish and over the course of the trainings learned a lot about the attitudes of managers toward Hispanics and became more involved in coaching troubled employees to be more productive. She became more passionate about the need for more such training in the corporate world.

Sheri has three surgeries 2001-2003

Sheri also had health challenges in these years. She had a bad case of gallstones and had to have her gall bladder removed. She also had a cyst in one of her breasts. After the doctors removed it, they found it to be benign. She then had three screws, present since 1987 bunion surgery, removed from her feet.

These scares didn't amount to much but caused a few problems when she lost a few days of work. I will admit the breast cyst concerned us for a month or two.

Otherwise both of us had excellent health and caught only an occasional cold.

Lee's new business, leaves Baker

About this time, I told my boss at Baker Newspaper Group I needed more time to develop my new coaching business. He agreed to let me work Monday, Wednesday and Friday for the same pay, which started my gradual disconnection from work.

About this time, Sheri and I went to Santa Barbara to visit her step-sister. I left my car in the parking garage for the weekend and we drove her car. On the way home, we forgot to stop and get my car.

Sunday night, I took to the Internet to find a new way to get to Beverly Hills without driving and discovered MetroLink and the Red Line subway, which got me close to the office. An express bus took me the rest of the way. From then on, I no longer drove from our home in Irvine to Beverly Hills. I took the train and bus for about three years and never drove to work again.

By2005 I worked two days a week for Baker and after our first seminar in 2006, I left for good. Seth Baker and I remained good friends until he passed away in Florida in July 2012.

Mexico Speeches 2003

In the Fall of 2002, Sheri received a strange email from Mexico. The organizers of a business conference wanted to know if she would speak. We had never heard of this group but when they said they would pay her way to Mexico and back, she accepted

After we discussed it, she called the girl back a few days later and asked if I could speak as well since then we could go together and travel further south after the conference.

Still, we had no ideas what our real roles would be. Then I looked the conference up on the Internet and what I discovered floored us.

We held two of the eight keynote speaker slots at the 36th International Business Conference at Tec de Monterrey, the MIT of Mexico, one of the most prestigious universities in Mexico. The room seated over 1,000 people.

Sheri asked if she could do a breakout session as well. "No," our hostess said, "those are for the mere lecturers. You, the Professors, do not do breakouts!"

Over the next several months, we prepared our speeches and made travel arrangements. The conference put us up at the El Presidente Hotel. When the big day arrived, we gave our speeches on a huge stage. To give you an idea of the class of speakers, I followed the man who had run on the PRI party ticket for President of Mexico in 2000, the first PRI candidate to lose an election in 70 years. Heady stuff.

After the conference, we flew to Guadalajara and then took a bus tour around central Mexico, through Morelia, Guanajuato, and other tourist havens. We ended up in Puebla for a visit with Sheri's Mexican family and a trip east to Vera Cruz, the seaport city near where Cortez landed in Mexico in 1521.

We join Toastmasters

My speaking career began over 25 years before my experience in Mexico. Now I wanted to do more speaking and do it on larger stages, like Monterrey. Sheri, a past member of Toastmasters in Hemet, suggested I join a club near Irvine, where we lived. She mentioned a club dedicated to authors, which I checked out and then joined.

One of the members, Richard Daugherty, a DTM, invited me to join his club in Mission Viejo. In November of 2003 I dived in and soon gave my first speech, the Icebreaker. One of the members said, "You are so good, why are you here?"

Good question but I had a better answer. Stage Time. I couldn't get a lot better without speaking a lot. Over the next year, I joined five clubs, spoke once or twice week, and finished the most advanced speaking level, and over 60 speeches, in less than 14 months, very fast for an organization where the average member speaks less than once a month.

In February 2005, I volunteered to become an Area Governor for the July 2005 to June 2006 year to finish all the requirements for my DTM.

A few months later, I met Arvee Robinson, a current Division Governor. We invented the Speak Your Way to Wealth seminar in May.

As part of my duties, I had to put on two speech contests, one in the fall and one in the Spring. By then Sheri and I had separated (I will tell you why in the next section) and I now lived in Placentia so I had a long drive. In the Fall of 2005, the District Governor announced he would give away the biggest trophy he could find to the Area Governor who put on the best Speech Contest in the Spring. After my mediocre Fall contest, I wanted to do better in the Spring. The result? In May 2006 at the Spring Conference, I walked away with a five-foot high trophy. It still graces my office, and is, indeed, one of the biggest trophies I have ever seen. My only regret is Sheri did not see me win it.

When my term ended June 30, I became a DTM, the highest honor the organization bestows on regular members, in two and one-half years, very fast for most people.

FOUR

The Waiting Game, Part 4 1980-1993

I have delayed writing this chapter for a while because I knew this long decade changed the rootless Sheri of the 70s into the mature, assured woman I met in 1993. It might be difficult to understand. This transition, filled with events, fascinated me because Sheri grew more familiar with each passing year until I saw the woman I met in 1993 appear. As I watch the pieces come together over these 13 years, I see attempts, a few successful, to deal with the childhood issues that held her back. I see her many friendships that lasted well into our marriage, some to the present day. I also see a confused mixture of public confidence and private lack of confidence, much of it caused by the lack of support she enjoyed as a child.

We hear about this all the time and as I have mentioned earlier, I never experienced it. Good parents were my normal.

After we married, I saw Sheri march ahead with confidence, then stumble backwards and crash in the moment when success appeared imminent. I cherished the vast amount of talent and skill she possessed and regretted the sad fact she never used it to best advantage.

On February 3, 1990, she wrote about this long decade in a clearer way. She had ups and downs, a breakup with her boyfriend, lost her mother and father, a new job, and a new spiritual sense. She says, "Insecure with success, will it last? Peaceful with self, feel good with job, buy house, OK to commit, five years housing, 2 ½ with new job, relationship OK now (with a drawn picture of a smiling face), have tools, not very defensive, don't have to be in the limelight, not important to be top dog. I must take care of self, I expect respect, maturity with relationships, exciting and mellow, self-assured, okay to detach."

She ended it with, "All is well, everything's in order."

Then, later in the same notebook, I found the following, dated April 14, 1990. "Just saw play *Emerald City*. It provoked a value search. I need to relate to myself and stay on purpose – to love myself and others unconditionally.

"What was wrong with Tom is what's wrong with me – fear of success. I try my damnedest to (screw) it up. It seems so precarious – the road to success – no, my staying on that road at all.

"I need to focus on me, a love affair with me, give myself the attention I want from someone else – cards, dates, sex, flattery, reassurance, encouragement, support, LOVE. Then I don't have unfulfilled expectations, agendas, etc. "

She stayed in the middle of this process until we met three years later. I wish I could have experienced this part of her life with her but at the same time, I realize we would never have worked out together.

I see her years in Hemet and Orange as exploration and centering years. She needed to mature before our relationship could happen. I will give you an outline of what happened but you don't need a lot of detail, job by job or speech by speech, since all of them are an endless string of one speech, one job, one boyfriend after another until in 1990 she bought her own house and no longer needed to depend on anyone else. As I go through this period, I see how much it meant to her to give up this house after only three years and move in with me in 1993.

Let's start with the escape from Arizona.

Move to Hemet, California

The first major break with her past came in late 1979 or early 1980, when she moved to Hemet, California with her then boyfriend. This took her out of the past into a fresh environment where she discovered she could flourish.

In rapid order, she applied for and got her MFCC license in California, went to work for a local hospital in Hemet, joined the local Toastmasters Club and became its president in July, and gave speeches all over the Hemet Valley area. Within a bit more than six months, she broke up with her boyfriend and moved into her own apartment.

Over the next five years she established herself in the community, set up her own business as a marriage and family counselor, and gave talks on relationships and alcoholism. She saved outlines of many of these talks and they still sound great.

She also went through a lot of counseling for her own problems of self-worth and adequacy. I think she took one of her most important steps when she joined Adult Children of

Alcoholics, and yes, she did present at one of their conferences. She stayed in the organization four and one-half years. Years later, I remember I attended a meeting with her in Orange County. She believed in their message of hope.

Hemet gave her time to explore. She traveled a lot, both to Mexico and around California, including a trip to San Francisco and the Central Valley, where she visited with relatives from her mother's side of the family.

I remember when we went to Idyllwild in April of 2015 for our personal retreat, we passed through Hemet. With great excitement, she showed me the hospital where she had worked and the apartment nearby where she lived, a small complex, five or six units along a path with small lawn areas in front. She lived on the ground floor near the carports with a huge tree above it. "It hasn't changed much," she said.

Her five years in Hemet set the tone for the rest of her life. She became a speaker, counselor, and consultant and made lots of friendships.

Sheri Loses her Parents

Her love-hate relationship with her parents continued in the Hemet years. She spent quite a bit of time with them in Arizona, I think always in the hope they would turn into the family she had never had. I remember she said a lot about them in the early years of our relationship.

She talked a lot about the loss of her connection to her past. She visited Arizona a lot, always with a tiny hope she might find feelings which didn't exist and had never existed, a sense of the loving, caring family she yearned for. Her mother drank too much to give it to her and her father played with too many women and built too many houses to pay much attention to her. She searched her whole life for connection to family.

This quest became more difficult because she had little close family to begin with. Her mother had one brother who never had children and her father had a brother who never married, so she had no first cousins. Her mother had no other children and her father had a son and a daughter she never knew very well. She had only her parents to hang on to.

In early 1983, her mother was diagnosed with pancreatic cancer. While she and Harold traveled in Spain in the summer of 1983, Willa had a stroke and after they came home, she had another stroke in November. Sheri kept an album of the cards and notes Willa got while in the hospital.

The first, dated November 20 says, "Sorry I'm not with you during this difficult time. I decided, and John Coglund agreed, I could be of more help when I return Thanksgiving. Brett's coming, too.

"Hope your recovery continues as well as it was when I was there. Coglund described you as 'rugged.' That's true. You've overcome and survived a lot of tough times.

"I hope you can find peace with this. I'm trying. See you soon." She signed it "Love and Strength, Sheri."

On November 22, she sent a card with a hummingbird on the cover and said, "Dear Willa – Thinking of you with loving thoughts, Love, Sheri."

Willa died of a sudden second stroke on December 8, 1983.

Nine months later, her father Bill Long had a sudden heart attack and died September 28, 1984 in Perris. California.

This twin loss of her most important family members devastated her. Even ten years later, she talked as if they had abandoned her, left her alone in the world. She even stayed away from her step-father for a while and had little contact with her step-sister Pam, who lived in the Houston, Texas area most of the 80s. For the first time she had nobody to fall back on. She would create or wreck her own life with no help.

Spiritual Life

Sheri never held strong religious views. In the 1970s, she described herself as agnostic. Part of this came from her mother's family. The Rehmes, strict Seventh-Day Adventists, raised their two children with no dancing, no drinking, no dating, and church every Sunday. Her mother rebelled as soon as she left home. Sheri thought her drinking started as an overreaction to her strict childhood. Church never played a part in Sheri's young life.

When she moved to Hemet, she discovered the Church of Religious Science. Before you jump to conclusions, this has no connection with other churches with "Science" in their names. This spiritual philosophy has since changed its name to the Centers for Spiritual Living.

Here she found the spiritual home she had sought. She never liked the Christian dogma her mother had grown up with and found the Science of Mind teachings of Ernest Holmes far more relevant to her life. She continued as a member the rest of her life.

I think one of the most attractive parts of the philosophy is it gives us control over our lives. What we think creates the life we lead, Holmes says. Its positive nature gave her strength to affirm her value and to continue to work for success. Through her final illness, it gave her the strength to survive the pain and uncertainty as she faced pancreatic cancer. I believe the positive attitude she kept through the last two years of her life gave her an additional six months to a year of good life, a gift I will be forever grateful for.

When she moved to Orange, California, she joined a new church founded by Rev. Jim Turrell in Costa Mesa and stayed a member the rest of her life. I will always remember Jim's final prayer by phone as her best friends and I stood around her bed in the moments after she passed and thank him for his gift to her of a strong spiritual practice she cherished for years.

Orange, California

In the first part of 1985, she and her boyfriend at the time, Tom, moved to Orange, California.

Within a year, she had gone to work for REACH EAP, an Employee Assistance Program in Anaheim, which provided counseling services to corporate clients.

At first, she attended the Huntington Beach church of Religious Science under Rev. Peggy Bassett, one of the largest churches in Orange County with close to 3,000 members and made friends who stayed with her the rest of her life. In 1987, she moved to Jim Turrell's church.

I know she traveled to Mexico and to northern California as well as to Arizona and a few other places these eight years.

She knew she had arrived when she purchased her own condo in Orange in early 1990. The notebook I quoted from earlier also has page after page of notes on how she planned to fix up her new home. She took pride in her home, which I visited within a week after we met.

At REACH, she worked with Hispanic employees at major companies like Kwikset, Nabisco, and the City of Anaheim because she spoke fluent Spanish. Here she discovered the vast divide between Hispanic employees and their bosses which led to poor communication and lost profits. Here began the germ of the idea she turned into a corporate consulting and training business.

In 1992 and 1993 she joined an internship program in Organization Development run by University Associates jumped into her new business with both feet.

By 1993, she had the tools for the rest of her career in place, the counseling license, Spanish language, organization development training, training room skills, and experience in corporate settings with high-level managers. Best of all, she made a difference. She made friends with many of these managers and as they moved on to different companies, they kept in touch and gave her business.

The same year, she had one more boyfriend who I believe she broke up with in late 1992. She wanted to find a new guy and when her friend Marlene Beno told her about her wedding in April 1993 and asked her to be Maid of Honor, Sheri jumped in with both feet.

Am I ever glad she did!

Part IV

2015

Wednesday,

The Fourth Day in November

Christmas Letter 1991

*1991 has been GREAT for me! I hope you've
realized as much and more self-understanding and
acceptance. I've been on this path of self-knowledge in
a new mode since Memorial Day when Tom and I
changed our five-year relationship from lovers to
friends. I've come to really enjoy my own company. I
feel very centered and content. The major renovations
on my nest are completed so I'm feeling more settled
and proud in my home. I've created beautiful
surroundings. The job continues to evolve and provide
lots of opportunities for personal growth. I went from
managing five to ten and building a new team. With
the transitions, I'm learning what my strengths are
and am molding the job to better utilize my natural,
well-developed talents of speaking, training, and
consulting with managers. I'm nurturing loving
relationships with friends and family – rebounded with
my step-father Harold in Yuma for Christmas. What a
gift! I'm going to continue giving myself the gift of
LOVE throughout '92. I hope you do, too!*
Love, Sheri Long
December 1991

ONE

Something Is Wrong,
Part 1,
Wednesday, November 4, 2015

When I got up Wednesday morning, I found Sheri still alive. Given what the nurses had said over the past two days, we had expected she might have slipped away overnight.

The morning nurse arrived at 8, peeked in the door and expressed surprise when she saw Sheri. When the RN arrived about 11 a.m., she looked at Sheri with surprise but added she had seen people hang on longer than expected. "I better arrange more nursing staff," she said. We agreed it might be a while, even into the weekend.

Sheri looked about the same as she had Monday and Tuesday mornings, similar breathing, moderate pain, discomfort, and anxiety.

I had heard at times like this, it might help to give the person permission to leave, which I had done to no avail for two days.

After I came back from lunch, Alice said, "I think we should try another approach." She explained, to my surprise, she had spiritual sensitivity to the thoughts of people, both alive and dead. I had heard of this but never experienced it. She also told us about her desire to do this kind of work with other dying patients. She calls it a death midwife. She talked about the classes she had taken and seminars she had participated in.

"Would you mind if I take her on a visualization journey?" she asked. "It is all metaphorical. I take her through two or three landmarks, help her drop burdens, and relax. It can help her to cross over on her own."

I told her to go ahead. We might as well. Yes, I had read about such events but real or not, I kept an agnostic view. I had never participated in a journey like this.

Alice sat near the head of the bed, called for Sheri to join her, and explained what she planned to do. "It is simple. We will cross a bridge across a stream, then cross a wide plain and climb to the top of a mountain, where you will be able to relax and prepare for the next step."

I listened and imagined the journey in my mind. It all went well. Sheri cooperated as Alice described each step. The process fascinated me. No trances, just a simple conversation with Sheri. It went so smooth we accepted it as normal no matter how unusual.

Alice reached the edge of the plain. "Sheri," she said, "now it is time to go up onto the mountain and relax to get ready for the next step."

Alice waited a moment, the looked startled. "Sheri stopped in her tracks like she was afraid of the mountain," she said. "Uh oh. She refused to go further. She told me no, she wasn't going any further."

We all looked at each other. Alice looked confused. "I've never had this happen before. I wonder what's wrong."

We had taken a sudden left turn, onto a bumpy road I had never anticipated, a road with no sign posts, surrounded by a thick impenetrable forest of surprise, rutted and little traveled. If this turn seems abrupt and surprising to you, imagine how it must have felt to us. Remember, through the next seven days, Sheri is unconscious on the hospital bed in the middle of our living room.

I accepted at face value that Sheri refused to cross over. What else could I do? She did say she didn't want to linger but then she also said she knew nothing existed on the other side. Was she wrong? Had she seen the other side? Did she face issues she never expected to face? Was it our imagination?

"Whatever it is," Alice said. "We can't ignore it."

I had never met this new Alice before. The Alice I knew worked as a corporate human resources manager, as far from this spiritual stuff as you can get.

I also saw a stronger and more assured Alice ready to take on a challenge. "I haven't done this very much," she said. "But it is what I want to do from here on."

I knew Sheri wanted to go. She had announced it to all of us at least three times. She had pointed out people in the room we couldn't see and even mentioned a guide.

A bit later in the afternoon, Alice said, "It's possible she needs to forgive people or ask forgiveness from them. I know a Hawaiian forgiveness exercise we could do."

She told us she had set up a spot on the other side, complete with a chair for Sheri and for those she needed to talk to. "It will go pretty fast," she said. "I won't know who she talks to or what she says but I will know when she is done. She will choose those she needs to call and is ready to do it."

Alice returned to the meeting place with Sheri. She explained to Sheri what we planned to do and Sheri agreed. Alice led us in a forgiveness chant and then set up a chair and asked Sheri to call everyone she wanted to forgive to come sit in the chair. Many spirits came and went very fast. We did not know who all of them are.

As she talked Sheri through the process. I thought to myself, "I wonder what this looks like?" So I took a bold step I had never thought to do in the past. I visualized the location, then in my mind stepped into it beside Sheri. I can't describe it any other way than to say I stood there, held her hand, and watched her go through the process. It felt like I stood on a dark coastline, or in a large cavern with a vaulted room, on sandy soil. I could feel Sheri's silent presence beside me. I guessed I shouldn't have gone there.

After we finished, I came back into the room and told Alice what I had done. After expressing surprise, she asked me to describe what I had seen. I told her about a sandy beach near a shoreline and the dark sky above and a stream and bridge off to the right. I also describe the chair. After I did, she looked surprised again and said. "With a few minor differences, that is what I saw as well."

"I was never sensitive to this stuff," I said.

"You are now," she said.

I realized I had stepped into unfamiliar territory. I had heard plenty about spiritual experiences, about the journey of the dying to the next world, even about people who sense the dead around them. I never had such an experience. A blank wall stood between me and the other world. Did it even exist? I didn't know.

"You're so good, you can come along with us on the journeys with Sheri," Alice said.

The routine part of this journey ended with those words. I wondered what new world wanted to open before me. I had no time to think about this new reality. In the moment, I accepted the truth of our situation and we moved forward.

The decision made, we attended to routine items. Later I had dinner, Sherree went out for the evening, and Alice brought the nurses up to date. Sheri didn't change much.

Alice talked a bit about her uncertainty as to what to do next. She'd taken a lot of training and had experience in these matters but Sheri took a different path. Her refusal to continue the journey confused us and left us unsure of the next step.

We decided to let Sheri process the day's events and encourage her. We also discussed what might block Sheri from leaving. I told Alice about her parents' alcoholism, which she had heard about, and about her step-father's passing and how these events felt like a betrayal to her.

Alice mentioned she knew of a shaman who might be able to help us and to keep her under consideration since who knew what might happen Thursday.

As I went to bed, I thought about the unsettling ramifications of the day's events. What a bizarre idea! An unknown block held Sheri back despite her expressed desire to not linger. The thought intrigued me. She lingered halfway to the other side. Why?

Then a most unusual thing happened. As I closed my eyes in the dark bedroom, I sensed a bright light around the edges where normally I saw only darkness. This bright light strengthened, then focused into a scene I had never seen before, still and quiet but with great beauty. I saw shadows of what might be buildings, green plants, and bright flowers. The scene appeared in what seemed to be an opening lens, revealing a world I had never visited.

I don't remember mentioning this to anyone during the next few days but began to look forward to the experience at night. The visions lasted for about a month after Sheri passed, then gradually faded.

TWO

Something Is Wrong, Part 2, September 1 to October 8, 2014

Dr. David Imagawa Takes Over

Neither Sheri nor I had ever heard of Dr. Imagawa. Why should we have? We had an intestinal issue. It turns out he came with a reputation – one of the world's top experts in diseases of the liver, pancreas and duodenum. He practiced out of the UC Irvine Medical Center in Orange, California, about 20 minutes from home, and as we found out later, had most of the sixth floor of the new medical building for his patients.

I remember the respect the doctors at Saddleback had for Dr. Imagawa. They admitted they did not have the expertise to work in this very sensitive part of the abdomen and he remained our best chance for a diagnosis. Sheri remembers they talked about him as a medical wizard, which he turned out to be.

Sheri went by ambulance to UCI. I met her and together we rode the elevator up the sixth floor. I had thought of Saddleback as a wonderful facility. I still do. However, UCI outclassed it. In addition to a spacious room, Sheri had no roommate and a nurses' station across the hall within easy reach.

We settled in and the orderlies arrived to give Sheri a chest x-ray and an electrocardiogram.

On Tuesday, Sept 2, Dr. Imagawa made his first appearance in her room, to explain they would do an upper GI exam under anesthesia the next day.

In the morning, he visited us again before the test. They wanted to get past the obstruction in the duodenum which kept her from eating. Then she went off to do the test.

Imagawa returned Thursday for more questions and to give us a preliminary result. He said they found, "Ulcerated tissue on the wall of the duodenum and inflammation, cause unknown." He said they did a biopsy but the results would not be available for a few days. He also added it did not look like cancer but if the biopsy came back as cancer they would have to do the Whipple surgery.

Friday, they inserted a new G-J Tube, which is both a stomach drain and a feeding tube, into her abdomen. It would stay in place until the stomach and intestine started to work again, if ever.

I didn't know at the time but the Whipple is VERY major surgery, six to 12 hours, where they take out the duodenum, part of the stomach and pancreas, and reroute several ducts, then tie the shortened intestine back to the stomach. Two to five percent die in the operation.

Imagawa also scheduled a family meeting for Saturday to discuss the options. At the meeting, he told us all the guidelines, made it clear he had a busy schedule, would not spend a lot of time with Sheri, and had a reputation for abruptness, which he confirmed. He said he kept up on all his patients, then outlined our options, which depended on how the biopsy came back. He described the duodenum, "It looks like a war zone, like a bomb went off in there."

The First Shoe Drops

Early Sunday morning, the biopsy came back. True to form, he walked into her room with his student doctors and informed her the test found cancer in the duodenum. "We don't know where it is centered but your only choice is to do the Whipple surgery," he said.

A few minutes later, I got a frantic phone call from her and rushed up to UCI Medical Center to help her sort out what had happened.

As we figured it out, wherever the cancer lurked, the Whipple would get it. Imagawa scheduled the surgery for September 26 because he wanted Sheri to stay in rehab a few weeks to build up her strength after the severe weight loss of the last weeks of August and all the procedures she had gone through.

Sherree Jolly and I spent a few days in search of rehabs near our home in Laguna Woods and recommended one by Saddleback Hospital. On September 12, they ambulanced her to the Laguna Hills Health and Rehabilitation Center for two weeks of recovery.

Sheri went into the recovery phase very upbeat about the possibility of a cure with the surgery. We had no reason to believe it wouldn't work so she looked forward to the stay in rehab and the surgery at the end of the month

A Sea Change in My Life

From August 10 to December 10, four months, except for 10 days from August 17 to 26, Sheri stayed either in the hospital or in rehab. The emergency room, go home, go back to the emergency room cycle ended. It now became hospital, rehab, hospital, rehab.

I lived alone at home with our dog Sally, a small Jack Russell, and our cats and visited her evenings with the dog after she entered rehab. I took care of the home. It got old fast. At least the nurses cared for her during the day so I had my days to myself. Still, I felt enormous stress. We didn't know, then thought we knew answer, got the answer and had no way to fix it. I felt a deep sense of loneliness after 20 years together. What a difficult adjustment! To see her with no energy, pain, and drugged with pain pills hurt. Rehab had people who cared for her, but the idea she belonged with all these ill and feeble people also hurt. I felt like high tide had rolled in with waves that rose and crashed on the rocks with no end in sight.

The first night I came home from the hospital without Sheri, I knew my life had changed. I sailed at sea without a compass. We had done so much together. The sudden lack of my partner took my direction away. Until I could decide where the new north in this new life lay, I struggled to make sense of what came next. Lack of a final diagnosis made this even more difficult. The waves under me rose and fell in random rhythm but in the black sea around us, direction became meaningless. Only the surgery we awaited could become the compass which would guide us out of this sea of uncertainty.

Around then, Bob Estrada called and wanted to have lunch. I enjoyed this breath of fresh air to get away even for a couple of hours and not talk about illness. To take care of yourself is much more than doing your work. It is also means you allow others to support you through the mess.

Rehab

Sheri settled into rehab. The first night she shared the room with another patient but the next day moved into another room which she had all to herself.

September 15, a poignant day, she called her boss at Paladin to tell her she had to terminate her contract since she would not be able to see patients for up to six months to a year. I know this devastating admission hurt her.

She also made a list of all her friends who needed to be notified about what had happened. We set up times when they could come visit but reserved the evening for me and Sally, the dog.

On September 17, to give you an idea of her positive mental attitude, she wrote:

"I'm grateful I have a FNP, Farideh, who really cares how I feel. She asked is pain better.

"I'm grateful I'm ambulatory and can sit alone in garden patio while it's cool from 7:15 to 8:30 a.m.

"I'm grateful nursing staff came out to the patio to take blood, give me breakfast or chat.

"I'm grateful I can see birds from my window onto the green patio.

"I'm grateful my room is BIG and I'm alone in it.

"I'm grateful for playful Ada who sings in Spanish that I know."

On Thursday, September 25, I drove her back to UCI for the surgery the next day. Sheri, happy and playful, expressed her eagerness for her nightmare to be over with the successful completion of the surgery and for recovery to begin.

Are We Ever Ready?

Pam Boswell, Sheri's step-sister, drove down from Santa Barbara for the surgery. They wheeled Sheri out early for tests and prep for surgery. Dr. Imagawa took us aside and warned us that the surgery would take from nine to twelve hours so to be sure to sit tight and not expect to hear from him until late afternoon.

At times, we are warned. Other times we never see the freight train before it hits us. Sheri and I and our friends expected a conclusion. After all, the doctor had identified the cancer, and had chosen the surgery, in her case The Whipple, confident he had it covered. We shared his confidence so I sat in the waiting room with Sheri's step-sister Pam, ready for a 12-hour marathon. I had work to do and she had plenty to read. The large waiting room had a door where the doctors entered and a small room where they delivered news, positive or negative, with the door closed. The hospital monitor on a post in the middle of the room gave the up-to-date status of each patient.

We settled in and watched patients, families and doctors enter and leave the room from time to time. I checked the monitor for Sheri's condition but saw little to report. Then in the distance, I saw a Japanese man dressed in a suit enter the room. Imagawa. Noon. Way too early. This is the first clue the surgery may not have gone as anticipated. Then I saw his expression. He's a serious guy but his sour glumness bothered me. He motioned us into the room, sat us down, and closed the door.

The News You Never Want to Hear

"It's bad," Dr. Imagawa said.

The words hit us like a lead brick. It took a moment to make sense of his words. Sheri's surgery promised to fix the problems with her digestion and remove the cancer from the duodenum – a great solution and the end of a traumatic six weeks.

"The cancer is in the pancreas and is wound around nerves and blood vessels. It is inoperable," he said.

I will never forget the trauma of this moment. It changed my life forever. I faced the stark reality I might lose my wife of 20 years. Would she ever live a normal life? Would she have tubes forever?

In the same instant, Pam and I looked at each other and she sobbed. I sat frozen, unable to act. I have no memory of the rest of the conversation. I couldn't let myself believe it. For six months, we had lived with solutions to crisis after crisis. Then suddenly we had the answer we feared, the answer we never prepared for.

As I struggled to wrap my thoughts around this news, I realized I would have to deliver this news to Sheri, my wife of 20 years, who had undergone this unsuccessful surgery.

I had no idea what to say. The last time I saw the inside of a hospital, I had my tonsils out at the age of 12. How could I stretch my mind around the idea my healthy young wife has pancreatic cancer, which could take her away forever? Words, just words. But which ones. In moments like this no words are adequate.

After Pam calmed down a bit, she composed herself and started to ask questions. My mind blanked. What can you think after the news your wife has an almost always fatal cancer and they can't take it out?

With the news still in our heads like a lead weight, Pam and I went back upstairs to Sheri's hospital room, where she lay on the bed in her room, groggy but awake.

I Ruin Sheri's Day

I have often wondered what it must be like to deliver bad health news. Doctors do it all the time and have many different methods. Since I had never dealt with major health problems, I had never had to tell a person close to me they might be sick, much less the disease might prove fatal. This thrust me into a position alien to my previous experiences.

At first, she slept, then started to wake up. I knew she wouldn't remember much for a few hours. After a while, she asked in a weak voice, "What happened?" I hesitated, then said, "It didn't go well. They couldn't take the tumor out." She listened and went back to sleep.

Half an hour later she woke up and said, "How did it go?" I repeated what I had said. She hadn't remembered a word I had said. She went back to sleep.

Her awareness grew the third time she woke up. I told her, "The surgery didn't go as well as we hoped. They couldn't take the tumor out." They became the most difficult words I ever said because this time I knew she would remember them. She accepted it at first but then became more and more frustrated.

Then I got a reaction I could not have predicted. Silence. Disbelief. Then acceptance of the news without understanding the consequences.

Life moved on, friends came to visit, the doctor visited, we discussed the situation, then got to the business of Sheri's food, pain medication, and sleep. Yes, it changes your life.

The Prognosis

I like our oncologist's comment on this the best, "I can tell you what has happened in the past. I cannot tell you what will happen to you in the future. Everyone is different. I can tell you what the survivors do, however." It is too bad most doctors don't put it this way.

Doctors used to cover up a bad prognosis, then because of complaints, they have gone the other direction of ensuring the patient knows in detail what lies ahead. This is almost as bad because we went from no prognosis to the worst.

For the first and last time, later in the morning, Sheri asked Dr. Imagawa about prognosis. Noted for his abrupt ways, he said the average is six months. He also said the chance of tumor shrinkage with chemotherapy ranked close to zero. He then said the stomach may never work again or could take six to 12 months to start up again. After he left, Sheri decided to never ask the question again. Yes, the statistics did not favor her but we would live in the moment from then on and take each step as it came. She would live each day and wake up for the next.

Before he left, she asked him to introduce her to one of his patients who had survived over four years. She then put up positive sayings in her hospital room, surrounded herself with cards from friends, and made up her own affirmation, that she knew her cells worked to create a perfect and healthy body. We never talked about statistics again.

The Inside Game

Sheri kept up a positive outlook but said little about her inner reactions. I can only talk about how I felt in the first days after the diagnosis.

Emotional devastation is the first problem. I remember the numb feeling that wouldn't go away when I realized I would be the one to give Sheri the unwelcome news.

I felt a moment of wild questioning. Why can't all the news be good? Why do we have to go through such trauma in life?

Then I realized we all face adversity and it makes us all stronger. To experience the challenge of my wife's pancreatic cancer made me stronger. I had to step up and do what I never thought I would have to do. I had to learn a whole new vocabulary about medicine and hospitals and insurance. This turned whatever I thought I knew about adversity on its head and roared at me from a new angle. I had no choice but to deal with it. I had to put the emotional problem behind me and work on the solutions.

The Best Attitude

The first step to reground yourself is to understand what you must deal with, then accept the worst possible outcome yet live as if the best possible is true.

We hear stories of long-term survivals. I know every person is different and every cancer is different. A few go away, many of them kill you. You never know at the start which you have.

Start with these facts: Bad news is never final. The statistics don't tell the full story. You will live the way you will live and die the way you will die and you will not know how either will happen until it happens.

Sheri and I turned our bad news to good news, to a new chapter in our lives. We intended to beat this intruder. Keep a positive attitude, eat right, and exercise. These keys keep the demon at bay. In a few cases, few and very far between, this will work. In most you will still die. Nobody beats this demon, except the few who do. Can we be one of those? Life will tell us and life never lies. We don't live in fear of death but in celebration of life. Death comes to us all, our appointed destiny. The time and date is never known to us. It up to us to live to the fullest every moment until the last instant.

The Survivor

Sheri made a clear first request to Dr. Imagawa. "Please introduce me to one of your pancreatic cancer survivors."

I had no idea what a five-year cancer survivor might look like. Tired, bent over, who knew? When we met Ruth, this 75-year-old dynamo and former truck driver looked ten years younger. She bubbled with enthusiasm, infectious bright eyes and a winning smile. Yet she had two chemotherapies, had liver cancer, had lost a lot of weight, and with a smile, said, "Hey, come visit me while I have chemo?"

Now let's be clear. Our cases were very different, Sheri's diagnosis allowed a very limited possibility of survival. Ruth also had Stage 4 cancer when doctors discovered it while she vacationed in Costa Rica. The doctors sent her home to die.

Dr. Imagawa performed successful Whipple surgery on her. Even with two recurrences of liver cancer, Ruth lived way past the usual survival rate. One could live with the demon. She survived because she became an active a participant in her treatment. To give up would kill her in a few months. To fight on would help but to keep her attitude in a mode of survival, watch her food intake, and keep fit remained critical to a longer survival time.

Ruth inspired Sheri. Doctors said she would live four to six months. She ended up a 13-month survivor, far beyond what the doctors expected.

Acute Recovery

I think Imagawa liked Sheri because he spent more time with us than with other patients in the days after the diagnosis. He wanted her to succeed despite the odds.

In the acute phase after surgery, doctors put her on heavy medication. The surgeons had opened her entire abdomen with an incision like the roof of a house (inverted v). The first day she dozed as she recovered from the anesthetic and wrapped her head around the new diagnosis we had revealed.

I spent a night and several of her girlfriends spent nights on a small bed in her room to keep her company. She didn't want to be alone for this part of the process. She recovered in the hospital for the next two weeks until she could walk around the hallways with Charlie (a mobile device that holds her bags of fluids) and the tubes. She depended on bags attached to Charlie for drink and food because her stomach still didn't work. She could take no food or water through her mouth at all. Her food entered by feeding tube and excess stomach fluid drained off through another tube.

We learned about new medicines, what the pancreas did and what it no longer did, how the digestive tract had changed and what all of it meant. The bottom line: Sheri now had two tubes, one drain for liver bile and a feeding tube so she could eat. Her digestive tract sagged and refused to function for quite a while. The doctors said it could take months to come back, or it might never recover. Sheri lay in bed and healed as all this activity spun out of control around her.

All this happened because the cancer had rendered her stomach and intestine inactive since the end of August. Dr. Imagawa had warned us several times it might take months for stomach function to return.

Every evening, I drove from Laguna Woods up to Orange, a half hour drive, to see her.

Dr. Imagawa released her to the same rehab facility near our house on October 8 so I lived five minutes away from her. She loved the private room they gave her.

THREE

Something Is Wrong,
Part 3,
July 2005 to August 2007

Speak Your Way to Wealth

Ten years ago, I attended a Marketing workshop put on by Adam Urbanski in Costa Mesa. At this event a friend of mine, Arvee Robinson, and I thought up the idea for a seminar on speaking which changed both our lives and led to my current career as a book editor and publisher. Arvee, a public speaking coach, wanted to get on larger stages such as Adam's event. I also wanted to get on stages to further my book coaching career. One problem. Nobody would invite us to be on their stages. When we looked at each other at the event 10 years ago, the answer became obvious. If they won't invite us to be on their stage, we'll set up our own stage and invite them to speak on ours! What better way to showcase ourselves to the best speakers in the business?

Because we had not spoken on many stages, we needed to figure out how to get good speakers on our stage. We couldn't make random calls. First, we asked ourselves who we already knew who knew us. Arvee had taken a class from James Malinchak and I knew Dottie Walters, one of the top female speakers in the country. We started with her. When we asked, they accepted. With great speakers on our stage, we could ask others who we did not know as well to join us. Because of who we already had, they accepted as well.

Once we had our speakers, we faced another challenge. How could we fill the room? With eight great speakers (including us), we would face horrible embarrassment if we put on an event with more speakers and staff than attendees. Time passed and the event came closer and still no attendees. We had to get busy. As late as three weeks before the event we had more speakers and staff than attendees. I talked to one of our speakers, who told me the story of his first event when he had all of 13 people in the room. Now he attracts hundreds to his events. We all start from a standstill. Not us, we vowed. We'd find attendees. We had no idea where.

With two weeks to go we had 20 people in the room. We went over everyone we knew. How could we get one of them to mail for us? The answer, of course, give the big guys a favor they wanted. We called and asked and offered and several important colleagues of ours sent email to their entire lists. The signups started. First a few, then a lot. We also reached out to our lists again, offered discounts and even gave a way a few free seats. The list grew but how many would show up? On the first day of the event, we set up for 100 people and about half an hour early, they began to filter in, first a few, then a lot. When we stepped on stage we had a full house. We learned marketing is the most important part of an event and to never wait so long to start again. It doesn't matter how great your speakers are if nobody comes to see them.

I Move Out

Two months after Arvee and I decided to do Speak Your Way to Wealth, Sheri asked me to come into her office. I felt depressed and my business had little income and she could sense it.

"I want to get divorced," she said.

At first it surprised me but I understood and didn't fight it. We didn't have money for two separate homes so I talked to my mother, Jessie Pound in Placentia, about moving in with her. At 87, she had lived alone since my father died in 1998 so she welcomed the company. I hadn't seen her much for a while so this would give me a chance to get much closer to her. At 87 she never got sick and had no more idea what the inside of a hospital looked like than I did. She even drove her tiny car around town.

She also had an extra room. I set up my computer and took up half the garage with the rest of my stuff from the garage in Irvine. All the books went into boxes in one of the back rooms. I moved.

In a lot of ways this proved an idyllic time. Arvee and I worked on the Speak Your Way to Wealth workshop one day a week and I dove into Toastmasters, where I joined five clubs, spoke up a storm, and served as area governor. My clubs met in South Orange County, 30 miles from my new home, not 10 or 12 from Irvine. Still, I made it work.

I had always gotten on well with my parents, unlike many people. Even though we had separated, Sheri still considered my mother to be family and would talk to her on occasion. Mother, a strong woman, active in her church, Placentia Presbyterian, had many friends in the community where she had lived for 57 years. She also had a cat, a stray who had moved into her back yard several years earlier. This cat refused to recognize anyone else even existed. The cat ignored me for two years.

I relaxed, took a lot of time for myself, worked two days a week in Beverly Hills and ran a few clients. It became a two-year retreat with little pressure. Sheri lived in the house, paid the house payment, all the bills, and took care of herself.

Yes, I missed her, but I also realized how much I had moved away from my past in the 12 years of our marriage. I did what she wanted and not what I wanted, which built a lot of stress. It took a few months to decompress and get back to work again.

While creating the speaking event, Arvee and I became close friends. She had a committed relationship so we never had a problem. After Sheri and I got together again, Arvee and Sheri became friends and the four of us got together from time to time to celebrate birthdays and anniversaries.

In the two years of our separation, I didn't date anybody, I decompressed and got myself back together again. I tend to use isolation to recover from stress so I made the best of this perfect opportunity. I will be forever grateful for the years I spent with my mother and for her non-critical acceptance of the situation.

Sheri traveled to China as part of a Long Beach Chamber of Commerce tour and she worked on her business both here in Orange County and with the maquiladora companies in Tijuana, where she presented leadership training in Spanish.

Divorce

Almost a year passed before I filed for divorce in the Orange County court. This tends to be a long, drawn-out process. We decided early on not to involve attorneys because we could not afford it and because it would only cause more strife.

After I filed, I did little to push this odd divorce along, almost as if an unseen hand held me (and her) back from completion.

We did keep in touch although many weeks could pass without contact. I used the time to decompress and figure out what had gone wrong. I think I always saw a possibility we might get back together but never mentioned it. Anyway, this separation and pseudo-divorce lasted for over two years.

While I lived with my Mom in Placentia, I worked on the Speak Your Way to Wealth event with Arvee. Our first event went off in August 2006. I enjoyed its success and gained new confidence from it. My mother attended and so did Sheri. In fact, she met Richard Villasana at the event and partnered with him in several business ventures in Mexico.

I only had one problem with living with mother. My room faced the back of the house. The neighbor, a recluse, played loud music all night a few feet across the driveway. I called the police many nights but they could do little about him since he lived on a large lot behind an eight-foot solid wood fence. This lesson in what people can get away with under certain circumstances gave me a new perspective on life.

We get Back Together and then tragedy

In early August 2007, as I talked with Sheri on the phone, she said, "Have you thought about getting back together?"

I admitted I had, which brought this answer, "Why didn't you tell me?"

It's hard to explain at this rather critical juncture but I must have done okay since we agreed to go ahead with the reconciliation.

Years later, after Sheri's diagnosis, I learned she had discussed the situation with her Mastermind group, and told them after a lot of thought and consideration she had realized "Lee is my man."

A week later, she attended my second Speak Your Way to Wealth, our most successful event and our first three-day event. My speech brought in a few sales to add to the huge amount of cash the other speakers generated.

The week after the event, in the euphoria of success, we decided I would move back home. I spent more time in Irvine and less in Placentia.

I stood on top of the world, with a great business and my marriage healed. Saturday afternoon, August 26, I hugged my 89-year-old mother and left to spend the night in Irvine with Sheri. The next morning, Sunday, we slept late, we went to church, and after we came home, she worked in the house while I went out in the patio.

My phone rang.

I answered.

"This is the Placentia Police Department," the official voice on the other end said. "Are you Leland Pound?"

"Yes," I said.

"I'm sorry to tell you this. Your mother, Jessie Pound, was in an accident."

I hesitated, then asked, "What happened?"

"A car hit her," he said. "She didn't make it."

Sheri came out a few minutes later.

"The Placentia Police just called," I said. "Mother had an accident. She's gone."

"Where do we go?" she asked as if she could not quite absorb the news.

"We have no place to go," I said. "She's gone."

It took Sheri a moment to process the information.

"We better go up to the house," she said, "and find out what happened."

"I need to call my sister Lynne first," I said. The news shocked her at first, but she said she and Garry, who lived in southwest Colorado, would leave, drive to Flagstaff, stay the night, then come the rest of the way the next day.

In Placentia, we stopped at the house, saw Mother's minister, and talked to the police about what had happened. She walked to church in the morning, as she always did, crossed a driveway at the Catholic Church, next door to her Presbyterian Church, and a car hit her and drove away. "Hit and run," the officer said.

By evening, the story had hit the local news and in the morning appeared in the Los Angeles Times. The headlines read variations of "89-year-old Woman Killed by Hit and Run Driver While Walking to Church."

We spent the day with the minister and at the house, where many friends and neighbors dropped in to express their condolences. I kept in touch with Lynne so I knew about when she would arrive, later about five.

A little before five, I saw a Channel 11 news van pull up out front. A few minutes later Lynne and Garry pulled up behind it and got out. All of us, along with the news crew and camera, went into the house and did a fast interview.

Lynne and I had a few minutes to confer before the lights went on and camera rolled. I'm sure it is still on the Internet. I know the story is indexed on Google. We put out a simple message to the hit and run driver to surrender before it got any worse. We didn't hate her, we didn't want revenge, we wanted closure.

Lynne stayed two weeks. We set up a garage sale and got rid of a lot of stuff but we still had 60 years' worth of accumulated stuff to clear out. We decided we couldn't do it anytime soon and turned to the idea of what to do next. If we wanted to rent the house, we had to remove all the contents. We had to repair it. We had to clear the outbuildings. Impossible.

The assistant minister at Mother's church contacted us and said they needed for a place to live for a few years. Lynne and I decided to make an offer. We would clear the house and put our possessions in the back buildings. He and his wife would live in the house and act as caretakers in return for reduced rent. He would get half of the garage and I would keep the other half.

Lynne and I became landlords. The minister moved in and stayed for four years. I had free storage and we got a steady income.

As soon as it all calmed down, I went to the County Clerk's office and filed a motion to cancel the divorce. Sheri and I started the second phase of our marriage on a fresh footing. We had no idea what lay ahead of us.

Part V

2015

Thursday,

The Fifth Day in November

Goodbye car. You've served me well. I've felt very comfortable and safe driving you. You've been maintenance free except regular expected stuff. No bad surprises like other cars. You've taken the dog(s) and me to the beach and put up with sandy feet, to kayaking and stinky duck muck clothes all over. You've taken me to Arizona, San Diego, Santa Barbara, San Francisco. You've taken pets to the vet and friends to play. You waited for me outside Tijuana. You've been loyal and trustworthy 6 years, through two houses, dollars up and down and now I let you go to serve someone else in your kind, thoughtful and easy way.

Sheri Long
July 23, 2013
On trading in her red Honda Civic
for a new red Kia Optima.

ONE

We Try Again,
Part 1,
Thursday, November 5, 2015

The shore is a place to enjoy. It is also a place to reflect on our lives, whether at the very beginning or the very end.

I like to think that before we take the ultimate step into eternity, we find a place to be alone with ourselves as we come to terms with who we are and what we have accomplished. The swish of the breakers we see tumble onto the sand with soothing regularity lets us meditate on who and what we are before we cross the plain that stretches away from the life we knew.

In this place, we can imagine that friends and relatives visit us from both sides, one group saying goodbye and another saying hello. Here we realize all is forgiven and we are welcome to complete our journey home. And in this knowledge, we rejoice, we celebrate, and we leave the shoreline, the boundary between here and there with no time or space or duration, and move on into the bright light of new life.

Sheri wanted to stay on the shoreline, a good short-term fix but under the circumstances a poor long-term strategy.

As I got up Thursday morning, Alice gave the new day nurse details of what needed to be done. I looked at Sheri. Same as the previous night. No change in breathing or level of consciousness.

"Did you hear a noise on the front porch last night?" Alice asked when I walked in.

"No," I said.

"I looked out this morning and noticed someone moved one of Sheri's ceramic frogs onto one of the chairs."

"Odd," I said.

Sherree and Alice and I went to Starbucks for breakfast and talked about the situation. Alice proposed we make one more run at the first journey to see if a change from mountain to a molehill might make a difference.

"Let's do it." I said.

After I got back from lunch, we talked about what might hold Sheri back. I knew she had alcoholic parents and had reserved her strongest resentment for her mother, but we couldn't see a problem there. We turned our attention to Sheri, sat beside her bed and held our hands over her to give her energy.

Then Chico, her favorite cat, jumped up on the bed and curled up next to her. He cuddled close, and closed his eyes as if in sleep, but sent energy her way as well. Cats can be so subtle but Alice saw it.

"He knows his job," she said. "He sends her energy too."

Chico cuddled next to Sheri, October, 7, 2015

We stood in silence around Sheri. I watched her and the cat. He lay in peaceful sleep, as if he belonged in this most natural place in the world.

My mind wandered until I saw this scene from Sheri's perspective in her in-between world. I remembered the scene from my last visit.

As we held our hands over the bed, I moved into a visualization of the spiritual realm where Sheri's consciousness lived now and where she slept in her comfortable bed in our safe meeting place.

This space carries an odd feeling. I felt no trance, only a simple vision in my brain or perhaps my eyes perceived another reality a few inches beyond normal perception. I felt present there even with my body rooted in my real living room, as if split between two realities.

I floated above her. From this perspective, I appeared to be at the top of the place where her spirit rested, below the ceiling. I felt like myself but to her I must have appeared like a star of light. I still poured energy down on her from my vantage point.

A short distance away, I noticed three bright rays of energy emanate from three bright stars in the black sky.

Of course, I thought, Sherree, Alice, and Chico. I could not see my own beam, the fourth bright light showering her from above. I flipped from the physical world into the spiritual world and back for a while, and existed in two places at once. Sheri lay in her metaphorical bed in this place, much as her body lay on the physical one in our living room, quiet, as if she needed to process the day's work. After a while, my vision faded back into temporal reality. We each lowered our hands and let her rest for the moment.

After dinner, Alice took Sheri on one more journey. They started across the bridge and onto the plain. Alice made the plain flat and the mountain a tiny hill. As they crossed the plain, Alice asked Sheri to put down her baggage. She does put down a few items.

As they approached the tiny hill, Alice asked Sheri to put down her burdens.

Sheri stopped, turned and said, "Don't you tell me what to do! I am not ready to go yet and don't push me. Quit standing around watching me."

Alice stopped, confused. "She read me out this time," she said. She returned Sheri to the meeting location and said, "Okay, it's time to let her process for a while."

TWO

We Try Again,
Part 2,
October 8 to December 10, 2014

When they wheeled Sheri in the door at the rehab center, we knew what to expect. Everyone sat in wheelchairs while Sheri walked. Most of the patients were in their eighties and nineties. Sheri is 67.

When the physical therapy guy saw her for the first time, she surprised him when she got out of bed under her own steam. "We don't know what to do with you," he said. "Most of our patients can't even get out of bed."

She still could not eat much although she attempted to take food by mouth. Much of it drained out of her stomach through the drain attached to a bag on her waist. She looked like a tube monster with the metal Charlie, the holder of the tubes, in tow everywhere she went.

We set up a schedule of friends who would keep her company during the day. I visited every evening and watched television with her. Her medication schedule meant the nurses awakened her at odd times each night to administer medications.

The Dog, the Healer

The rehab policy allowed animals in the rooms, which made rehab bearable. As soon as we discovered this, I began to bring Sally, our little Jack Russell, with me in the evenings.

Sally got so excited to go to rehab she ran to the car and couldn't wait to get in every night. A hyper little girl, she loved to be included. In the room, she would jump up on the bed and cuddle with Sheri while we watched TV. Sally gave Sheri great comfort and a little bit of home for the months we spent in rehab.

Sheri spent October, November, and early December there, a few miles from home. The staff gave her great care. After a few weeks, they gave her leave to visit the house a few times and for doctor appointments. Sally helped get her through this traumatic period. I'm not sure what we would have done without our loving little pup.

In Sheri's Own Words

While in rehab, Sheri wrote quite a lot about her condition and feelings. In this chapter, I will let her words speak for themselves. The routine itself didn't change much for those two months. Friends in the day, lots of cards and letters, me and Sally in the evening, exercise, physical therapy, medication after medication, and the occasional crisis. It is not necessary to go through all the detail. Then important part is how Sheri herself viewed her situation.

Sheri's Journal, October 19, 2014

I'm scared. What am I scared of?

I will request bedside commode to be safe for night time peeing. I'm afraid of falling.

God grant me the Serenity to accept the things I cannot change;
The Courage to change the things I can;
The Wisdom to know the difference.

I know I can encourage and gently get my stomach to use the new pathway. The Ensure and milk feel like they're going down the new pathway as I gently sip reasonable amounts. I will manage my time well – being and the love and the concern of all my loved ones who are counting on me to conquer my fears and thrive through this challenge.

It can be done.

I know I can do this.

Sheri's Journal, October 21, 2014

Hi dear friends and family!

I welcome your visits! Please help me keep them to 30-60 minutes together so we can preserve my precious energy for my healing. Please call or text Linda so we don't double book your visits.

Update on Big Surgery:

The big surgery on 9/26 didn't come out the way we anticipated. There was a little critter in there playing footsie with my pancreas, some nerves and blood vessels so they had to leave him in there until we can shrink him down to manageable size and extract him. Later they gave him an ugly name: Pancreatic Cancer.

So I spent about 12 days at UCI recovering from the surgery and have been at the Rehab Center since 10/8. It's the same Rehab Center where I spent a couple of weeks getting strong enuf for the big surgery so I got a very warm welcome from everyone.

I mostly have a good time here, exercising in P.T., gaining balance and other skills in occupational therapy, and enjoying games, art, and movies in activities.

Everyone knows me here cuz I zip down the hallways with Charlie, my tall, handsome, slender IV pole, while most patients wheel or get wheeled around here.

When my lab results show I am no longer anemic and malnourished, I'll go home to continue rebuilding my health so I can benefit from about three months of chemotherapy.

When chemotherapy shrinks the unwelcomed critter, we'll get it evicted.

It's sounding like Groundhog Day!

In May surgery for adrenal tumor;

In September, surgery for gut:

In a few months, surgery for critter.

COPING SKILLS: I'm taking it one day or 1 minute at a time, reading spiritual stuff, practicing keeping my head in a positive place, writing gratitude lists, journaling, talking to wonderful friends (like you), resting, doing what doctors and medical professionals advise and appreciating life more than ever before.

Love you, Sheri.

PS I feel so loved by you as I look around my room which is wallpapered with your cheerful cards and decorated with lots of colorful flowers and snuggle-soft stuffed animals.

Sheri's Journal, October 27, 2014

I am grateful there is a syrup with 17 grams protein in a "shot glass."

I'm grateful I have so many caring friends.

I'm grateful I have a dedicated husband.

I'm grateful Chico remembers me.

I'm grateful Joan is watering and caring for my side garden.

I'm grateful Pam squeezed in a visit with me.

I'm grateful I have a sisty.

I'm grateful I have a sis Yvette.

Sheri's Journal, October 31, 2014

Dr. K asked me for a decision on my goals for treatment.

Talked to Rodney, who seemed perturbed that she asked me this.

What's she thinking??I need her on my side. Or, do I? It would be nice but the most important person I need on my side is me.

So I love Charlie cuz he carries the sustenance that nurtures me. He supports the machine that delivers my food.

I love all the nurses who do their best to deliver good care to me. I'm glad the CNAs want to be helpful.

I truly appreciate Jaciento's getting the good-tasting Prostat for me and writing my name on it.

I'm taking more of my care into my own hands. I'll set my cell alarm to unclamp at night.

I want to tell Dr. K she needs to share my vision and goals.

Sheri's Journal, November 1, 2014

Just called Ruth. She said to remember this is temporary, everything is in Divine order.

I just spent two hours at home on the couch watching funny recorded programs. All the pets greeted me. Chico licked my hand thoroughly and lovingly. Being there made me realize how important it is to me to get home from rehab.

I believe going home for visits will move my recovery along faster. The stomach will feel it's old atmosphere where it is comfy and happy.

She'll relax and start using the new passageway sooner cuz she believes we're going home soon where we can thrive.

Everything is in Divine Order! It's all working for my good. I have so much love around them. So many friends – loving friends – generous friends. I'm seeing new sides of them – gentle sweet generosity.

Ruthie said she saw my specialness the moment she looked into my eyes. She knows I'm one of the ones who make it. I've got what it takes.

Rodney basically said the same thing, comparing my go get'em approach to the residents he tries to convince to get out of bed to get well. He sees them as wanting someone to take care of them when they go home. He sees me as wanting to go home to take care of myself.

I've noticed I'm probably the only person who voluntarily participates in PT exercise and seeks out my PTA rather than waiting for them to hunt me down.

Sheri's Journal, November 8, 2014

My stomach is divinely guided to process food through its brand new shiny freeway.

Through Divine Guidance my stomach processes all types of food through its brand new shiny freeway.

My stomach loves to eat! It processes all my favorite foods through the new plumbing.

I love to eat! My stomach gladly digests all my favorite foods and sends them down the new plumbing.

My stomach gladly processes all the food I give it and sends it down the new plumbing.

My stomach welcomes and uses the improved plumbing system.

My stomach is thrilled with the new plumbing.

My stomach embraces the new plumbing system.

My stomach accepts the new plumbing system.

My stomach opens up to the new plumbing system and processes all types of food through the new pathway.

The new plumbing opens up and accepts all types of food.

Sheri's Journal, November 10, 2014

It's such a beautiful day. Sun's shining, cool breeze gently wiggles the flag.

I'm grateful for the red geranium who's poking his head out of the hedge, the dull hedge with the red flower poked through. I'm grateful the gardener respects the flower by leaving it there and not cutting it down to the hedge's outline.

I'm sooooo grateful Tina, LVN, diluted and put the Prostat down the J tube. Boom! Done! Don't have to suffer through the day, figuring out how to disguise the flavor so I can stomach it.

Sheri's Journal, November 12, 2014

I don't let my past run me.

Fear – Willa's torturing me driving on left lane of incoming traffic.

Enuf is enuf!

Yes, own it. Stuff happened to me. However, it's not who I am.

ETOH (alcohol) meant more to my parents than I did.

They don't run my backstory any more. I live in today. No fear. What's gonna be is gonna.

Sheri's Journal, November 13, 2014

Sheri's Plea for a WII.

Sheri has had to much fun exercising on the Wii game at the Rehab Center that she would like to have one at home.

The Rehab Center has had many exercise options through physical and occupational therapy which she will not have at home. The Wii *game offers a wide range of fun exercise activities to keep Sheri strong for upcoming chemotherapy and more surgeries.*

Do you know anyone who has a Wii console they're not using anymore and games?

I go to Frontier in San Diego in November

From November 11 to 17, I went to Clinton Swaine's Frontier Trainings advanced classes in San Diego. This included the big one, the courses where we create a special three-part contract we say every time we walk on stage at Frontier.

I felt a bittersweet emotion because Sheri could not be with me for the first time. She encouraged me to take the time away from the medical situation and enjoy myself for the first time in months.

I am glad she did because I came home energized and ready to take on whatever would come up in the future.

The courses stretched me in so many ways I can't remember them all. One segment, the physical, included running, exercises, and sore muscles. I found out I could run, not as fast as I wanted but with a lot of endurance.

The other segment, the mental part, led to the completion of impossible tasks. I can't go into any detail because the games are confidential but at one point I and three other guys got dressed up as the Rock Group KISS (look them up to see how we looked) and performed until the audience believed we were KISS. It didn't take long. I still have the photo of me in my makeup.

I am so grateful to Clinton for the way he took care of Sheri at the two sessions we did attend earlier in the year. I know she wanted to be at the training with me because the family and camaraderie meant so much to her.

Insurance Part 1

By now we knew Sheri had an incurable disease. The doctors gave her six months to live. Back in 2010, we took out a life insurance policy on her with a rider that the company would accelerate payment of the $135,000 face amount if this happened.

In rehab one day, we looked at each other and Sheri said, "What about the life insurance policy?"

"We can file for the payout," I said with a smile.

It took a little while for the payout to come through but it meant we had no more money problems, for good. The problem of how to keep the income up would go away in time for Sheri to come home.

Leaving Rehab

At first, we expected Sheri to come home in late November but then she contracted a bowel infection and had to go onto an antibiotic drip for two weeks.

In early December, she put out this note to everyone.

"THE GOOD NEWS!

"I am going home on Wednesday, December 10. I'm to know that chemo starts on Tuesday, December 16. Treatments will be only one hour, enough time to relax but not so long I will get bored. You know me!

"The doctor expects minimal to no side effects but understandably I'm still apprehensive about how my body and mind are going to react to chemo. I disciplined myself to focus on the positive (a positive outcome). Please do the same."

Insurance Part 2

Chemo can create a horrible financial mess. We already knew the insurance would pay only about a third of the cost and chemotherapy drugs could run over $6,000 per month. Yikes.

I was a bit apprehensive when the oncologist called to tell us how much our copay would run. The first number, a nine, scared me. A nine and a zero followed – with a decimal point before the second nine. I was ecstatic. $9.90 per session for chemo. We had dodged another bullet.

The Challenge of Illness

Sheri's pain, discouragement and fatigue meant she needed all the encouragement I could give her as she prepared to come home.

Her friends contributed a lot and visited her often but I found no answer to how to cope. Everyone is different and will face different challenges. We had to take care of each other now and not let the circumstances rob us. It is easy to go nuts when faced with such challenges.

We had to work together as a couple to get through this. No you or me situation. Both of us worked as a team to deal with an issue in the most intimate way possible, as one.

For couples, such a crisis is not about you or me, it is about us. Both of us are part of the problem and both are part of the solution. We work together and think about our partner first, then take actions based on what is best for both of us. We each have our tasks and we each act to support the other.

Every act of encouragement and love makes each of our lives better. The selfless performance of the necessary tasks, a trip to the pharmacy, a drive to doctor appointments, my presence when needed, my ear when needed, moved us both closer to the ultimate solution, whatever it is.

The goal is to make life livable under the worst of circumstances. If we make it hell for each other, we destroy the best part of each of us. If we make it heaven, we create a new powerful intimacy we will treasure forever.

I enjoy my friends today. I love to feel loved. I don't give power to negative judgmental thoughts. Love empowers and fuels me through the day. I stay consciously in a state of love.

Sheri Long
March 13, 2013

THREE

We Try Again, Part 3, August 2007 to December 2008

We are Back Together

We faced the world together. With all our parental family ties gone, we had no close relatives nearby to hang out with.

Do you remember late 2007? The overheated real estate market started to cool off but houses still cost a lot and the go-go economy still ran full steam ahead. Nobody expected a crash.

We had refinanced the house and paid off our credit cards earlier in the year and had $50,000 in the bank, earmarked for a rebuild of the kitchen. Since the day we bought the house, Sheri wanted a new kitchen so as soon as I moved back in, we began to plan. She hired a designer, got estimates, and got to work. By the end of 2007, we had spent most of the $50,000 but we had a beautiful kitchen, new appliances, and very little debt. We both made good money. We also still had savings. We had one shadow on the horizon: Our house payment would go up in 2011. But, like many assumed in those days, the economy would take care of it.

Arvee and I planned our next seminar for August 24, 2008. After the first two we knew we had a good deal. Sales had soared in 2007 and we worked on an amazing lineup for the future.

Sheri's business continues to grow

Sheri's business did well, too. She had strong clients, offered training classes to large corporations and saw quite a few private clients. It all added up to great cash flow. We bulled our way through 2008 with bright prospects ahead. It was time to take the world by storm. Yes, we had a big expense nut. It would get bigger in a few years but why worry? We lived in a strong economy with a hot real estate market and enjoyed life. We saw hints but no obvious signs of a problem.

The Market Crashes

August 2008 arrived. Arvee and I had a huge crowd and a wonderful lineup of speakers for our event. This would be our best year yet. We would have lots of people with money to spend and in those days, seminar attendees spent a lot on programs.

Sheri had several good jobs lined up. I left Baker Newspaper Group in 2006 because of the hot seminar business and my book clients took more and more time. We saw even more clients in the pipeline.

Then in mid-August Lehman Brothers went bankrupt. In one day, the economy started to collapse, the real estate market froze, the stock market lost half its value in a few days, and loose credit ended.

I don't think we realized the magnitude of the crisis at first and compared it to other downturns of the past. As the days passed, it became clear we faced a major crisis. We held the seminar as expected but many people didn't show up and most of those who did didn't buy much. A couple of us, me included, had the best sales days we had ever had but in the next month, many of those cancelled so the good sales drifted away.

Then towards September, we knew real estate values had crashed. I heard of cities like Las Vegas where homes lost more than half their value in a few days. Buyers vanished, sales fell through as loans could no longer be made, and a cold wind blew in. Irvine fared better than most areas but the value of our home dropped by over 15%, which meant we now owed more than the house's resale value and in this financial climate who knew how long it might take for prices to come back.

As we moved into Christmas season and beyond, it became clear the country had avoided a major depression but we also knew the recession had spread around the world. We had no haven.

The $50,000 we spent on the kitchen assumed greater importance but of course we could not recover it. Sheri's corporate clients complained of tight funds and postponed training sessions. Suddenly, the increase in our house payment became very important. If this recession lasted very long we might not have the money for a bigger payment and of course, who would want to put more money, all of it interest, into a house worth less than we owed on it.

It became a test of my financial ability to keep all this afloat. I worked the savings and the credit cards and house payments, and kept it all current but as the months dragged on, the balances rose and to prospects looked even bleaker.

Part VI

2015

Friday,

The Sixth Day in November

Creative Intelligence is omni-powerful. So am I. I know my value and I powerfully express it. My inner knowing gives me confidence in my inherent value. I convey it confidently. There is no truth in devaluing myself. The TRUTH is I have preciously valuable gifts to offer and I value them enough to charge enough. I value my time to charge enough. I love myself. I love others. We make a mutually satisfying arrangement. I'm glad to have this philosophy to support my dealings. I let go and let God.

Sheri Long
October 15, 2012

ONE

Breakthrough, Part 1, Friday, November 6, 2015

Friday turned into more of a waiting day than I had expected. I got up early and showered and by 8 a.m. arrived in the kitchen to get breakfast. Our day nurse arrived about 8 and settled in.

Alice said, "I still can't figure out what happened yesterday. All I know is I need help with Sheri." She again mentioned the Shaman, a friend of a friend who knew a lot more about how to handle Sheri's reluctance to cross over.

"I would like to call her, if it is all right with you," she said.

"Go ahead," I said.

Alice called the Shaman, who told her she had a full day scheduled and could she call back after five p.m. We agreed.

I heard a knock on the door. I answered and found our neighbor across the sidewalk, Diane. She came in and asked,

"Did you hear anyone on the porch the last two nights about 2:30 a.m.?"

Alice and Sherree looked at each other and both said no. Both slept on the couches in the living room, very close to the front porch. I knew if anyone made noise outside, they would hear it.

Diane said, "I got up Wednesday night about 2:30 and glanced out the window at your front porch. I saw a woman seated in one of the chairs. She had dark hair and a white face and appeared to be very cold. I thought she might be a homeless person but they are rare inside the Laguna Woods gates."

We all said we had heard no sounds.

When she got up the next morning, she told us, she wondered more about the woman. She came up with a test, move one of the ceramic frogs on the porch into the middle of the chair and see if it moved the next night.

"We noticed the frog in a new place and wondered why," Alice said.

Diane said, "Last night I saw the woman seated again in the same chair and when I checked this morning the frog still sat in the same place I left it. I had to come over and tell you about this."

As you can see, the odd events started like a whisper from the Universe, a foreshadow of unique events ahead.

The whisper got a little louder a few minutes later when Sheri's friend Joy from Dana Point (about 20 minutes away on the coast, showed up at the front door.

"Sheri woke me up last night three times and told me to come up here this morning," she said. "So here I am. What's the matter?"

Alice told her about the previous day's spiritual journey and its abrupt end. "We still don't know what's up but this is very strange."

After they both left, we chatted with the nurse about Sheri's condition. We all agreed she was one of the best nurses we had.

When she checked the oxygen monitor (which looks like a large clothespin) on Sheri's finger, she saw a heartbeat of about 135 and an oxygen level held in the high 90% range, higher than might be expected for a person in Sheri's condition.

We checked the record. Her heart rate stayed at this same level day after day. How unusual!

Alice told her Sheri manipulated the heart and oxygen levels to communicate with us. A raise in the oxygen would indicate yes and drop would indicate no.

The nurse said a person couldn't have control over the monitor because it measures the external amount on the finger.

She pulled the monitor off Sheri's finger, let it reset to zero, then placed it on her finger, where it registered the expected levels. She then placed it on another of Sheri's fingers on her other hand. The oxygen percentage, which should never exceed 100%, shot up to 500%, stayed about 10 seconds, then dropped back to Sheri's standard of 135 heart rate and 98% oxygen.

She shook her head and went back to the desk.

At 11 a.m., our lead case nurse, arrived and again expressed surprise Sheri hung on to life unchanged. We talked about the level of care, which had improved a lot. She said it should not take much longer. Sheri had not eaten in over a week and the body can last only so long. She increased the morphine drip and added a drip tube for Ativan to make Sheri more comfortable.

By this time, we had the nursing situation under control. Most of the nurses we wanted around took longer shifts and came back more often. However, she said the process had lasted longer than expected and the nurses were burned out. A couple had put in 16 hours in a row. After she left, Alice and Sherree told me to get out of the house and get lunch, which I did. I got back about 2:30 and we all talked in turn to Sheri, while we monitored the situation.

Sheri's minister Jim Turrell and his wife Patty came by about 4 and stayed about an hour. After they left we waited for Alice's phone to ring.

Surprise and the Beginning of Peace

At 5:30 p.m. the Shaman called and Alice gave her a brief account of what had happened. After Alice explained it in detail, the Shaman asked her to take hold of Sheri's feet to establish a connection with her through Alice and the phone.

"Okay," Alice said. She pulled her chair over to the end of the bed a few feet away and put one hand on Sheri's feet and the other on the phone.

She listened for a few minutes, then looked up in surprise. "She says Sheri's mother is blocking her from going over to the other side. She's acting like an evil, disconnected spirit, the bad part split off from the good part." She listened another moment. "She says almost everybody crosses over to the other side. Sheri's mother never did. She still lingers there."

This surprise made sense. Sheri's mother had died over 30 years before and given the circumstances of her childhood and how much she had resented them and held onto them for so many years, this could happen.

Alice asked the Shaman how we got Sheri past this. She said later she expected the Shaman to ask her to put the phone by

Sheri's ear and lead her through the necessary steps to clear this block.

The Shaman said, "I'm not. You will lead her through this."

Alice said, "But I don't know how."

The Shaman said, "I hope you take good notes." Then she launched into a detailed list of instructions while Alice wrote page after page of notes.

When she finished, she hung up the phone and gathered Sherree and I together. "We need candles and red ribbon and white roses. This must be fixed before Sheri passes or she may be stuck in limbo with her mother. We have to do it now."

We rushed around and found a red piece of ribbon, one white candle and carnations. Sherree found a candle holder and I found matches. We used the carnations in place of the other candles we didn't have.

Alice tied one end of the red ribbon to her wrist and the other to Sherree's. "This is a dangerous place and if I get stuck you can use the ribbon to pull me back to reality."

The nurse, scheduled until 8 p.m., joined us in the circle around Sheri's bed. The three of us held the carnations while Alice sat close to the head of the bed to talk into Sheri's ear.

Before we started, Alice called in guards or sentinels, all of them masters from many spiritual traditions, four female and four male, to stand guard around the four corners of the bed. I don't mention their names because their presence is important, not the tradition with which they are connected here on Earth.

Alice said we would go to a different place this time, a multi-level matrix where Sheri's lives and connections all came together. The matrix has two levels, the first level, where Sherree and I will stay, and a second level, where Sheri and Alice will go and which swarms with all of Sheri's life connections. Alice tells us not to go to the second level because it is too dangerous.

On the second level, Sheri will face and heal her parental relationships.

Alice, Sherree and I go to the place where we met Sheri the day before and call her in. She explains the next steps and gets Sheri's consent. All of us then move toward the matrix, visible now a short distance away.

We walk up the path to the matrix, shrouded in darkness. At the first level, Alice and Sheri leave us behind and move up to the second level. As they approach the center of the matrix, five sparks of light emerge from the darkness and hover about them. Four of them merge into two. Alice later told us these were the good and not as good parts of her father and mother, now reunited so they could complete their relationship with Sheri. Sheri and her mother and father have two options, to complete the relationship or to continue it into the future. Both parties must agree.

Sheri talks first with her mother. We can hear no words, we see the conversation, we see the nods, and then we see Sheri and her mother decide to part and Sheri cuts the connection. Her mother fades into the surrounding darkness, free. Sheri then turns to face her father, who she had sworn to never forgive many times in her life. They talk, come to agreement, and then she cuts the cord and allows him to fade into the darkness.

Sheri then faces her step-father Harold. At first, she wants to cut the cord on the relationship because of her anger at him for leaving her when he passed away a decade earlier. He says to her, "No, we have more work to do together." They finally agree and Sheri keeps him in her life.

She has now forgiven her mother and father and made peace with them. As renewed souls, they are now free to pursue their next mission.

Alice and Sheri turn and come down the stairs to the first level, followed by her step-father, who stands with us as we return to Sheri's cozy resting place. We all watch as she falls into a deep sleep and then return to the house exhausted but exhilarated.

About 6:30, Alice said, "I'm exhausted. I need a big fat steak." We drive over to the Lone Star Steak House in Laguna Hills, where she bought big steak dinners for Sherree and I.

While we ate, the Shaman called and asked two more questions, "Was Sheri ever married before?" and "Did Sheri like Christmas?" I told Alice yes, a short marriage 40 years ago. It had no significance. And yes, Sheri loved Christmas.

Christmas in November

Most people have no idea a person prone on a bed with their eyes closed can have experiences. It's time in this story to stow away our preconceptions and listen with an open mind. I'm about to tell you a Christmas story. It takes place in another dimension and nobody has ever told it before. Don't turn away. You might learn a lesson.

Sherree, Alice and I stood in the living room after the second call from the Shaman. As we looked at Sheri unconscious on her hospital bed, I thought, yes, Sheri did love Christmas, her favorite holiday of the year. She got to decorate, give presents, throw a party, be the center of attention, play with family, all in an atmosphere of celebration.

I said, "Christmas meant a lot more to her. She couldn't wait for it. It's so sad she won't be able to celebrate it this year."

Alice said, "Can you think of a special gift you would like to give her?"

"Of course," I said.

"Yes," Sherree said.

Alice said, "How about if we do a Christmas party for Sheri? Right now!"

The vision flashed through my mind. We step into another dimension, where Sheri is vibrant and alive. She creates a Christmas made of thought, and we decorate it with ornaments of gossamer. We give gifts that were never made. She gives gifts that don't exist. We treasure them forever. When we step back into reality, all is as before. No tree, no gifts, Sheri on the bed. But we know in our secret hearts we have given her joy beyond knowing. And that makes us happy.

"Let's do it," I said.

"First," Alice said, "we have to set the stage. Sheri would never go to a party dressed like this."

We found a favorite green dress and laid it over her. I found her favorite necklace and bracelets and we graced her body with them. She looked beautiful, as if ready to transcend every possible boundary.

What a normal situation! Sheri lay on the bed in her living room a few feet from where her Christmas tree landed every December. I could sense the decorations already hung on it and knew what they looked like.

Sherree, Alice and I gathered around her bed and Alice led the visualization as we slipped into Sheri's private place, where we gathered by the long seashore and across from the bridge over the river.

Alice called for Sheri to come to us and when she arrived, she said, "Sheri, we have brought gifts and will celebrate

Christmas with you." Sheri, ecstatic, grinned and twirled around a few times. Alice told her to decorate the area any way she wished so she created a tall Christmas tree bright with lights and shiny ornaments with a red star on top. Garlands of green surrounded us.

We placed our colorful wrapped gifts around the tree and Sheri opened them one by one.

I gave her a bright red fuzzy jacket to keep her warm. She tried it on and danced around with a smile on her face.

Sherree gave her a red lapel pin with a reclining kitten on it.

Alice also gave her a gift.

We all admired the gifts for a while, then Alice motioned for us to leave. As we prepared to leave, Sheri said, "No, wait. I have gifts for you!"

We returned to see what she had thought up for us. They would be special because these were the last Christmas gifts she would ever give. I expected no less from her. And she didn't disappoint.

She gave Alice a beautiful crystal ball she could use in her chosen profession.

She gave Sherree a black, carved beaded necklace and bracelet and said, "Now you look sexy!"

She gave me a pocket watch with Mickey Mouse hands which did not work and said, "Here we have no time or space. This is the gift of eternity."

We accepted and admired our gifts, hugged each other, opened our eyes and returned to the living room. The place felt different, more peaceful, warmer, and filled with love.

We had done it! We had healed her and given her a wonderful send off to the next world. She might be ready to go.

Or was she?

We all know and accept there's a Divine Spirit in and through EVERYTHING, like air on earth. It's pervasive. We enjoy it and need it to survive. Divine Spirit is our true nature. I declare my health is in Divine Order. I stay focused on this truth and it multiplies each time I seek professional advice and take positive action. I keep my focus on recovery from this diagnosis because that's the TRUTH. There is no power in entertaining thoughts about someone else's experience of loss. I actively see myself doing all the healthy activities I love to do, Zumba, kayaking, dancing, walking long ways, swimming, learning pickleball, etc. I'm so grateful for this truth I gladly keep this focus. I know it's already a done deal so I let go and enjoy. So'tis.

Sheri Long
August 3, 2015
11 p.m.

TWO

Breakthrough,
Part 2: Home at Last,
December 2014 to October 2015

Becoming a Caregiver

I never expected to become a caregiver. Even when Sheri became ill and had surgery in early 2014, I took care of her in the few days of recuperation after she came home from surgery.

Even in July, after she stayed in the hospital about 10 days she came home and took care of herself. She worked, saw clients. and drove herself when necessary through the end of the month.

In August, her hospital stay lasted 11 days. My slow journey to caregiver ramped up near the end of August, when she had trouble eating and we landed in the hospital again.

The pattern settled into time in the hospital, time at home, time in the hospital.

Then from August 27 to December 10, she lived in rehab or the hospital, not at home. I spent most of my days by myself, at work or with the animals. When needed, I went to infrequent doctor's appointments. I spent evenings with her either in the hospital or the rehab. The medical facility and their nurses took care of all medications.

By December, I had some idea how her medications and tube feeding and drains worked but not until a few days before she came home did I even practice those functions. I figured when she came home a few hours a day might be enough to take care of her.

I had even, over the summer and fall, cut back on my individual clients because I knew I might have less time to serve them. I concentrated on the Writers Workshop classes and Sheri.

Sheri Comes Home

When Sheri arrived at home December 10, I assumed the role of caregiver and stepped into an unfamiliar landscape filled with invisible but dangerous holes you cannot see, flowers filled with secret poisons, and odd plants behind familiar shapes.

I became the full-time caregiver, my tasks the same as the nurses in the hospital and rehab had performed for four months. I got no time off. The pills must be managed, tube feeding managed, bags cleaned, pain handled, and doctor's appointments kept. I managed the first few days well but then realized the work never gets done, the animals need attention too, and worse, the business needs attention, now relegated to the last hour before bedtime. People have gone mad in this situation.

As a caregiver, you juggle the personal and professional parts of your life. An encrusted shell keeps the two apart. In one the compass is clear and direct and in the other it is confused and directionless. To step between these two shells is like a step from a raft lost at sea to a sturdy platform with one direction. It is easy to compartmentalize life like this with a hard shell around each, but you can lose touch with your true direction in life.

To become available to both your spouse and your clients, you break the shell apart, acknowledge the two compasses, and ask for help from those you care about the most. They will guide you as you reconcile the two incompatible parts of your life. As a professional, you become more sensitive to your clients' needs and as a caregiver you invent direction where none exists. Soon the compasses merge and the shell drops away, leaving life with a new sense of meaning.

Very early I realized I had to take care of my needs as well as my wife's. Statistics show many caregivers die before the person they take care of because of stress. Take breaks, get out of the house, find friends to take over for a while, make time for work. My time no longer belonged to me. Routine tasks took so much time I had little energy left. This frustrated me.

The Equipment Invasion

The whole look and feel of the house changed after Sheri came home. First, the kitchen ceased its normal function as a kitchen and became a medical center with pill bottles and solutions lined up in neat rows on the counter. A tall pole with several hanging bags became a permanent fixture wherever Sheri stopped for a moment. I had seen the nurses use syringes before but when I handled them, I noticed the feel of the plastic in my hand, soft yet hard, the resistance when I pushed solutions into Sheri's feeding tube and the frustration when it got stopped up. The house started to smell like a nursing home. I wondered when we would get our normal house back. I never expected it to take seven months before normality returned.

I needed a compass to guide me in the right direction through such an unfamiliar minefield. Within a day, I created a medication spreadsheet first on paper then on the computer which became my compass to guide me as I provided her with medications on a very complex schedule.

I remember one day, I think in January, when one of Sheri's girlfriends told her to take responsibility for her own care and not throw it all on me. I knew she needed to do this but never brought it up. She reacted with an effort to take some of the burden off me. Instead of the default to think sick, she went out more. Months later, she got off methadone and started to drive, which took even more burden off.

Chemotherapy Part 1

We went to our first appointment with Dr. Wagner on November 24, before she came home, to discuss chemotherapy. Sheri had a lot of questions for him, the most important about cost. I heard horror stories of thousands of dollars per month.

This visit including quite a revelation. He talked about Sheri's comfort and about how little we could shrink the tumor.

This meeting upset Sheri so much we made another appointment.

"I need to know you are on the same page as I am, and I need you to show a positive attitude about this process. Otherwise I can't work with you," she said at the appointment.

He made a couple of key points. "First, I can only tell you history, not predict outcomes," he said. Second, a positive attitude, good nutrition and exercise show up in everyone who survives for any length of time. He told her he had survived cancer himself and knew how discouraged one could get.

"It is very important for you have a decent quality of life through this. You don't want to be miserable," he added.

As it turned out, the first chemo would be Gemcidabene, also known as Gemzar, the drug of choice for pancreatic cancer. Our copay would be $9.90 per treatment. We both breathed a sigh of relief.

She would have infusions at the doctor's office one time a week for one hour for seven weeks, then take a one-week break, then three weeks on and one off. Then the doctors would take a CAT scan to see whether the treatment worked.

We decided to start chemo on Tuesday, December 23. She would have a lab test the Friday before to make sure her blood levels would allow the next infusion.

On December 5, she sat down with our friend Diane Estrada to talk about chemotherapy. Diane had gone through it with her own cancer a year or so earlier.

Sheri's notes say, "Talk to my body before chemo. Tell the cells what to expect. 'We're going to be blown to smithereens. You know exactly what to do to come back from this attack 100 times faster than before.' Also talk to cancer cells: 'You're going to be going away with love. I've got what I need to know. Thank you.' The healing light of God takes care of me and you. Look good, feel better, find some free wigs."

Sheri went through the first chemo session and waited for the side effects to arrive. They must have taken a different train because they never showed up. A week, two weeks, three, she still had hair and no other effects.

Sheri continues to gain strength

I won't go into all the details of the next few months since they aren't needed. By March, Sheri felt much better, had gained a lot of energy and, although she still had the feeding tube, her digestive system worked well again. She even started to eat solid food. In May, the liver drain tube came out and she started to take more time off the feeding tube.

Even the pain subsided and the doctors took her off the methadone fir the first time since her surgery.

Spirit Mountain Retreat

Late in April, we went on a four-day personal retreat in Idyllwild near Mt. San Jacinto east of Los Angeles. Our fee included rooms and food. We could think, rest, read, and explore all we wanted. I did most of the exploration because Sheri could still not exercise much.

On April 19, 2015 Sheri wrote the following, "*I'm torn between actively dealing with the critter and ignoring it, focusing on the quality of life I want. I want: 1. A normal healthy functioning digestive tract. 2. 100% energy – so I feel confident kayaking, Zumba full out, play all day without stopping to rest, sleep easily eight hours or more so I feel rested and healed. 3: No pain – get up and go.*"

The next day, still at Spirit Mountain, she wrote, "*I'm bored. Lee is teaching his online writers workshop. He gets a charge out of doing it/sharing his expertise. I'm Jealous. I need to think how I can share my expertise. Just the book isn't enough. I want to conduct a workshop. I love sharing my special knowledge to managers who really care about their Hispanic workforce. I know people who care:*

Kazuyo, Ted and Terry, Roger's Poultry, Chris Fuller, Diana Alvarado, her boss, Richard Villasana, Art Vigil, Loren Meglide, Nancy, Oscar…"

I remember her excitement when this idea came up. She wrote, *"What's the most beneficial thing I can do with this writing time? I just thought of something fun I could do. Laughter Yoga Workshop at Spirit Mountain: Laughter and Love, Monday Tuesday nights and leave Wednesday. Ask Alice to do Yoga in a.m."*

She sketched out the plan, even made a day by day schedule. I think given more time and better health, she might have pulled it off.

Chemotherapy Part 2

Sheri had started chemotherapy in December of 2014 and after several months she had no reaction to it except for vomiting. She kept her hair and felt energetic. However, after 12 sessions on Gemzar, we did a CAT scan and found the lesions on her liver had gotten larger. Dr. Wagner told us we would need to go on a different chemo, this time an expensive one. He recommended a service which paid a large part of our deductible so it didn't cost us much.

We started the new chemo, Tarseva, in June, and still no side effects except for a slight rash, which vanished after a few days. We had more trouble healing up the last hole when the doctors took out her stomach feeding tube in July.

Tarseva cost more, $6,000 a month. So far, we are out all of $5 per month, the rest paid by insurance and a special program.

Live Day by Day

(Written in June 2015) Most of the scars have healed, the tubes are out, and the medical supplies are stored away. We embark on the next phase. We enjoy the day to day power of our lives. Sheri plans a trip to Santa Barbara this week to visit her step-sister. We will take a week vacation to the mountains of Arizona in August to hang out away from the chaos. The routine of medicines and chemo, exercise and doctor's appointments, times of pain and times of fun will continue, one day at a time. Sheri has new clothes and a new bathing suit to fit her new svelte figure and I have new shirts she found while she bought her stuff. We have grown so much closer together as we have taken this journey. Life shows no sign of a slowdown. The best is still to come.

As I write this, (July 2015) Sheri is in Big Bear with her friend Sherree, a great getaway to the mountains. They are on a three-day retreat complete with tubes and medications. At this point we are 18 months into this journey with pancreatic cancer, with no end in sight. In a way, this is good because in most cases of this kind, we see a clear end in sight and it arrives very fast.

To work together on such a serious illness has its ups and downs.

The Lull Before the Storm

As I write the rest of this chapter, it is November 9, 2016, the one-year anniversary of Sheri's passing. I'm having a sunset dinner at Romeo Cucina, just off the beach in Laguna Beach. A spectacular sunset over Catalina Island greeted me this evening.

Romeo is a special place for us. We ate here often and Sheri threw her 60th birthday bash here. The back area where we celebrated is empty now. On that day, it hosted a festive gathering of 40 topped off with a gelato cake from Dolce Gelato next door.

I'm having tagliatelle meatballs, a tasty concoction. It is not on my diet but I will take most of it home.

Why did I come here after a months-long writing blackout? Laguna Beach and Romeo help me remember Sheri at her best as I write the next segment of her story, the last few months of her life.

I had written much of this six months ago but then I found the journal she kept from May to early September 2015. My version was antiseptic, with little emotion. I may not have been ready to express the emotion of those days back then. Since then I have attended several meetings of a grief group at Saddleback Hospital and redecorated the house to make it more my own.

As I read through the journal, I decided that the raw emotion here is the story of those months and that it is best if she tells the story herself in her own words with little interruption from me.

It begins on a high note, the gradual recovery that surprised all the doctors in April, Frontier Trainings in June, and the removal of all her tubes in July. At the end of that month, she was as near normal as she would ever be. This long, exhausting process was replaced with plans for the rest of the year and celebration at how well her recovery had gone.

Dr. Imagawa had given her four to six months to live at the end of September 2014. Here we were in July, nine months later, tubes out, pain medication at a minimum, eating real food. She felt good, though a bit tired at times, and pain was minimal and bearable.

We celebrated.

Laguna Beach seems to be my muse. Eating gelato at Dolce brings back so many memories of the good days, the fun days, when we hung out with friends, laughed on the beach, and looked forward to a grand future.

There was no gelato in July 2015, no great plan. We lived in the knowledge that she was already past the doctor's expected survival time, that we might not see the new year together. And yet, it seemed that we might, just might.

Still, it is devastating when the first signs of decline appear. A bit more pain medication, more tired, harder to get food down. We ignore them, hope they will go away, keep our spirits up, do not allow the illness to take over our lives even as it worked in an inexorable march to take hers.

I put off writing this section, or better yet rewriting it. The first version was very terse and unemotional and was written when I was too fragile to go any deeper. So here is her story of the last six months, most of it in her own words until they stopped flowing, then in mine.

We lived as if we were suspended over an abyss by an invisible hand that could drop us at any moment. You have already read about what happened when the hand finally dropped us on November 1. These last months are an inspiring story of grace and poise in the face of extinction. In that descent through pain and uncertainty, she packed all the life she had into a wild last ride and let go only when she was ready.

Sheri's Journal, April 26, 2015

I had a glimpse of myself as normal in the mirror. Déjà vu sort of feeling. I'm in the same house, same marriage, etc. I'm still myself. Doctors look at me as a diagnosis and what they have experienced with that. I'm a new experience. I'm breaking records, changing history and their experience. I'm myself, no one else. I'm living!! a normal life. I'm so grateful for what I can do. I walked a mile in 20 minutes.

That's more than I did before. I want to finish the book to feel normal and like I'm contributing. I want to bring joy to people.

I'm grateful for this loving kitty; for Lee's devotion; for neighbors; for girlfriends' Haagen Dasz; TV; Mary Hardesty; Spirit Mountain; for LIFE. I'm alive!

Sheri's Journal May 13, 2015

What do I want treatment for? Pounds up, pain down, tube feedings work, sound restful sleep, positive attitude up, exercise, moving comfortably as celebration, energy up. Take gratitude time every day. Truth is there's power greater than the fact of condition. Opposite of fear=confidence. Higher power within us. Qualities I want to experience.

When resenting I'm using energy I could use positively. What would I rather do? Acknowledge how I feel and move on to truth.

Spend time on the goodness of who Sheri is. Bring spirit into whatever we're doing. Ask spirit what to do i.e call someone who needs life, movie, expose myself to beauty-Rogers, Sherman Gardens.

Go to nature place I haven't been to shift mindset – NEW.

Beautiful gift of life – Gratitude.

Beautiful fresh spirit!

Relationship with spirit deepens daily – share with others.

Thank you. Let go and enjoy! She treats daily.

Sheri's Journal, May 17, 2015

I'm grateful for:

Joy's wisdom

Sherree's trust and confidence

Lee's dedicated caring, help, willingness to get food and do things for me like flush.

Friends like Kay who visit me

Critters who snuggle with me and walk with me.

My ability to walk one mile in 20 minutes or less

My cozy nest where I can turn on the light to write my gratitude list without disturbing Lee

Joy and others praise my courage and positive attitude toward my health. David H said long term positive happy cheerful attitude. Dr Wagner thrilled with lab results pleased with my progress. It's nice to have patients survive and overcome cancer.

I don't yell from the mountain tops like ---. I just live my life in the healthiest way possible or that I want to do each day.

Sheri's Journal May 21-23, 2015

Slept and went to Sue's party. A.M. bile drain removed

Grateful for Norco, Frank McCourt's books, cat who warms me, sweet next bed, Lee's understanding, my ability to sleep thru night.

Frontier, May 23 to June 1, 2015

Late in May, we went to Frontier again, her first session since the previous summer. She again took her sleeping bag and used it often when she became tired. One of the classes trained us to speak so she gave several talks about her attitudes toward the cancer. I still have one of them recorded. In another of the courses, she got to dress up as a star and present her costume to the entire group. Here are her thoughts on that week:

May 23, 2015

I'm grateful for friends like Sooz, Denise, Michael; my ability to go out with them; going to Frontier Trainings; Clinton Swaine; Heather's lodging at $10 per might; Norco, sleeping bag in room; my courage to go lie down; my caring for myself; Shadow sleeping with me

May 24, 2015

I'm grateful for: a friendly place to stay that's understanding and accepting of my "Charlie"; my pain has gone away from 5/5 Norco; Lee who gets my stuff I need.

May 25, 2015

I'm grateful for Clinton's hugs and caring; powerful experiential learning – earthquake; my ability to participate and not participate when I need to rest; to see old friends and make new ones.

May 26, 2015

I'm grateful for being able to support myself by speaking to group about my situation and ask for them to support Lee if it comes to that. I'm grateful they raised their hands and Bokkie confirmed she cares about us Frontier or not. I'm grateful my discomfort eased this a.m. I appreciate Julie Ann's help and caring.

I'm grateful Susan offered two nights.

I've learned I don't like writing procedures and systems and I don't like long drawn-out building projects that I check out and settle for a mundane task rather than share my creativity.

I will speak up and request we share the fun creative artistic tasks.

So do I want to be a leader in Lords of Plantasia? I'm scared of being fired. So what? Not the first or last.

June 3, 2015

I'm grateful for Disneyland with Clinton and gang Monday June 1. I had soooo much fun! I was able to last 10 hours by driving electric vehicle and napping at first aid. I'm grateful for sharing Julie Ann's awe and joy as first timer.

June: The High Point of Recovery

Sheri was still taking pain meds in June after we returned from Frontier at the end of May. On June 4, Sherree invited her to take a few days, just the two of them, in Big Bear.

Lee and Sheri walking in Heisler Park, Laguna Beach, July 1, 2015

Dr. Wagner was ecstatic that her liver function was almost normal and was satisfied with her weight. A few days later, another doctor let her stop some other medications. She could still drive. Best of all, her childhood friend from Arizona invited us to stay at her cabin near Payson for a week or so, maybe in August.

On June 12, she was hit by major pain and the pain doctors increased her methadone dose to 5 milligrams. At the time, this seemed like a small setback but we had good news, the end of tube feeding and her ability to eat real food for the first time in months.

June 24, 2015

Need to call Gale re cabin dates. Now that I don't need tube feeding, it's easier to imagine cuz less hassle. I keep waiting for weight to stabilize. It's good. Just do it! Gale closes the cabin in mid-October. We were thinking August.

I feel fine. Good quality of life. Had Norco 6 a.m. so no pain now. I plan to eat and walk one mile with Sally. I forgot to weigh – 123.

From Science of Mind magazine: Ram Dass says healing means allowing what is to move us closer to GOD.

Dr. Geiger: Medical fact not the truth – I'm connected to Source that doesn't know illness.

June 28, 2015

I'm grateful for good friends who came to my rescue today.

For my persistent, reliable belief that I'm healing just the way I should. I'm learning to be more humble and adjust my activities according to my well-being.

About this time, we received notice that Carolyn, a long-time friend of Sheri's, had passed away after fighting cancer for several years. The service was scheduled for July 1.

June 30, 2015

What do I want to say at Carolyn's service? Known her 25 years, enjoyed her sense of humor, deep spirituality, very helpful in talking through my personal problems, lived with Lee and me 15 years ago.

July 1, 2015

Carolyn's service was nice. Jim seemed distracted. I didn't get emotional catharsis I expected. I'm sorry she's gone. We shared a special bond and common language with 12 step and church philosophies. I'm grateful for the richness she added to my life.

G'night girlfriend.

July 5, 2015

Lately it was harder to be with Carolyn. Consumed by her illness and <u>trying</u> to be so positive; dominating air space.

Am I avoiding plans for my death? I'll probably feel better when I write up ceremony.

Music – Peruvian –relaxing love beat (beginning).

Song In This Very Room (set mood) sing along Jean (unify in spirit) Jim tell my life outline and how he knew me. Mara tell our relationship. Others eulogize me.

We reached the height of recovery on July 5, when Dr. Lee removed the last tube from Sheri's stomach. It left a small hole in her abdomen into the stomach which the doctor said would heal in a few days. It didn't. I can't tell you how frustrating it was to have to deal with this draining that refused to heal. I had to change the dressing two or three times a day and the frustration as it calmed down, seemed to heal, then opened again was constant. The Big Bear trip stayed on schedule, erupting stoma or not.

July 13, 2015

I've been too preoccupied with GJ stoma eruptions and management to journal. I'll go to Big Bear tomorrow, keeping this in perspective so that I have fun.

I'm grateful I'm alive! Keeping the grateful perspective – loving Lee's support and friends.

I'm so glad Sherree invited me to join her. She knew the risks with my unpredictable situation. She's a good friend who's very willing to stop and do whatever's needed to get it done.

G'nite… z z z

July 14, 2015

My thermostat (internal) is playing games on me. I'm getting sweaty. I don't want to get hot when I'm there – falling asleep and awakening hot, sweating. What is the deal? I CAN control my bodily and energy.

Sheri and Sherree in Big Bear, July 15, 2015

July 15, 2015

Sherree and I had a good time in Big Bear. She was agreeable and patient with my wound care. She respected and inquired about my energy level. We laughed at the stoma's eruption and didn't take it too seriously. I would have liked to stay another night.

I hope Carolyn had someone she could talk deeply and openly with about her death.

I'm aware that I've been critical of others which means I'm not happy with me. What? I'm hurting and bitching, letting loss of hope creep in, like, "Will I be able to do some things I want to do?" What quality of life do I want? I don't want to be a bitchy, distant, uncaring self-centered person. I want to have something loving and helpful to offer people I care about. Poor Lee! It's so hard to be in the caregiver role. It tests all his "competence" buttons. He's learning and growing.

July 16, 2015

I feel fine – in perfect health. I plan to acknowledge each moment of healthy feeling. That is my TRUE nature.

I'm so very GRATEFUL for all my accumulated moments of health. As I acknowledge them they expand with pride. They puff up their "chests" and show off for the world to see. Yay!

July 19, 2015

I love the rain on my metal roof. So enchantingly relaxing and hypnotic. I feel like I am in another world and this one can't get to me.

The next day we discovered a new TV series (to us) *Hart of Dixie*, a light relationship comedy about a young female New York lawyer who moves to small-town Alabama and the cultural shocks and wonders she meets. Sheri fell in love with it so I had to join Netflix to get the back three years we missed and we started binge watching, sometimes two or three episodes at night.

July 23, 2016
Lee's 70th birthday!
Told him Happy Birthday 82 times.
Watched Hart of Dixie five hours.
Reconnected with church friends
I sang birthday to Lee

July 24, 2015
Day after Lee's 70th and Sue's 64(?).
Need to get goofy gifts for Ruthe, Lee, etc.
I read what a man I don't know wrote about SOM. He claimed that Earnest Holmes had clarity to take out the religious God-fearing stuff to know it is what we make of it – how we interpret it for our lives. He said Earnest said fear is man-made and we can change our minds.

July 25, 2015
At our 11:45 a.m. appointment Dr. Wm Wallace, surgeon, told me I look like a million bucks and held out his arms to hug me.
Lee said I'm a miracle.
Yippee!!!
I feel like a million bucks until I get tired – usually afternoons.
Many times, I've heard medical professionals say I look healthy and normal. Yay!!!
This 1:30 a.m. I awoke feeling like I could not move my arms. What a relief when I moved my shoulders. It still felt like a dream so I kept moving my arms.
I told Dr. Wallace I felt proud to have diagnosis of Stage 4 Pancreatic Cancer with Metastasis to the Liver cuz I know one day I'll say "I've recovered from Stage 4 …!!
I'm a miracle NOW!
(About midnight) Welbutrin withdrawal? Grouchy, self-centered, critical. When I awoke last night (4 a.m.?) I had the sensation I wasn't going to be able to move. And then realized it was back pain at my waist, which could have been caused by posture, lack of exercise, etc.

July 26, 2015
"You look like a million bucks!" Dr. Wm. Wallace. Focus on that! I'm very grateful for his observation.

It seems to be this quiet early hour that I think negative scary thoughts.

The cats love this time of day. All their senses are heightened with outdoor critters teasing them.

July 27, 2015 wee hours of a.m.
My Bucket List
Galapagos
Peace of Mind
Complete recovery from diagnosis of "Pancreatic Cancer Stage IV with Metastases to the Liver" asap.
San Diego Zoo
Unconditional Love

July 27, 2015, almost midnight
Grateful for:
Pam's eager invitation
Train ride
Fun things to do, like H2O pencils
Good friends
Norco

July 28, 2015 At Pam's, wee Wednesday a.m. hours
Jean Houston said most of our thots are the same. "Yes," I agree. I want more new thots to propel me forward away from pain into comfortable health – free of fear that "disease" is increasing.
Sleep! Fears born of fatigue and loneliness so sleep!

July 28, 2015 midnight
SOM book: "Science must justify faith." Hmmm, interesting.

Falling asleep …
I'm grateful for:
My sisty who just said she loves me.
Her listening to my fears about cancer
Taking me to movie
Being OK with my long naps
Appetite and she prepares lots of food
My paying for movie for both of us
Mary's understanding.

August 2, 2015 wee hours of a.m.
I'm grateful for:
Books Mary sent – easy read and lifted me up
Eating lots of small meals
Avocados
Attended lunch and party
Participated in house blessing.

August 5, 2015
Too tired to treat.

August 13, 2015
*I'm afraid I'm dying. Dr. Granlund PCP said she could feel my
liver like it's swollen. My right side hurts. I'm having trouble eating.
Dr. Wagner said keeping my weight up is super important.*

*Dr. Geiger, Saddleback Hospitalist, said tumor larger and more
lesions for prepare yourself and get Hospice.*

We'll see what Dr. Wagner says today.

I've had night sweats so got two towels, top and bottom.

*God grant me the Serenity to accept the things I cannot change,
the Courage to change the things I can and the Wisdom to know the
difference.*

August 16, 2015

Turning a page and making a break thru take time, getting used to. I felt so certain and so confident yet I flip-flopped. Depends on how I feel, physically.

August 20, 2015

Goodness and bright light is everywhere. It guides me and everyone else who so chooses. It's a part of me like I'm a part of the light. I declare perfect divine outcomes from the visit with Dr. Wagner. Lee and Joy (maybe Pam.) I know the Universe provides the perfect right tools for my perfect divine health. When Dr. W expresses doubt in the future, I remind him we follow a white light of Divinity. I inform him I'm grateful for my belief in Divine order and everything is in Divine Order. I let go and bask in the confident knowledge that everything is always in Divine Order. So 'tis.

Pam and Sheri's sculpture garden one year later

August 22, 2015

Pam left 2 pm ish after lunch with Yvette and me. Great having all of us together.

Pam and I had a great time building two succulent sculpture gardens.

Sheri in her nest with Sally the dog and Shadow the cat, July 2015

August 23, 2015

Yvette commiserated with my vacillating that's of, "Will I die from this cancer or will I get through these hoops and survive it?" She suggested living one day at a time. I want to continually know I am one of the small percent who makes it.

August 24, 2015, 1:30 a.m.

At the same time shrink the pancreatic tumor to nothing, 0, nada.

Lots of people, friends, are counting on my total recovery from pancreatic cancer Stage 4 with metastasis to the liver.

(Writes Serenity Prayer again)

G'nite. Zzzz

August 27, 2015
Falling asleep so going to sleep.

September 3, 2015
What do I want for thanks:
Weight up 2.5 pounds toward goal
Guilt-free releasing of Sally to a welcoming nurturing home that serves both needs.
Free, comfortable and confident to do the activities I love to do.
Thought with feeling = prayer
Spirit relaxes and moves my gut so it's natural movement in peace, ease and perfect outcome.

September 9, 2015
One year! 9/27/15
Health and wholeness now
Juicy enthusiasm
Release Lee to own experience, embrace trust, celebrate learning.
Internal knowing of how to be present in Spirit no matter what's going on.
Bring consciousness forward to connection to God/Spirit that unlimited joy in every cell we say THANK YOU. We know the TRUTH. TRUST
I forgot. Plug back in!
Grannies on Camino Blog. (Her spiritual partner's blog. Check it out.)

Sheri's last journal ends here, two months to the day before she made her final transition.

She Loses strength

By August Sheri had begun to lose strength. I suppose I didn't want to see it since she had made such a remarkable recovery from the surgery and had gotten all the tubes out. She had an exciting time and performed well at Frontier in June. I believed we had quite a bit of time left.

We saw ominous signs. Sheri complained about more pain and every time we went to the pain doctors, they increased the dosages. She never complained much, a murmur about pain from time to time. She took Norco and morphine as needed but the intervals got less and less and the times she had to take both increased.

I also noticed she had more difficulty with food and had started to complain of fullness in her abdomen. Still, she looked healthy even though she did nap more and more and got out of bed less and less. She also stopped driving about this time because she didn't feel comfortable in traffic.

Then at the end of August, we had a conversation in her office. She said we had too many animals and they tired her out too much. We had a dog Sally (a Jack Russel) and three cats. She said she no longer had the energy to participate in Sally's care. Sally barked at every noise, day and night and she couldn't handle it.

We agreed we could no longer care for Sally and looked up Russell rescue operations in Southern California. We signed the papers to give her up, a sad day for both of us. The week before we left for Arizona in mid-September, the rescue people took her away.

I remember the day not for the sadness but for the quiet. Sheri could no longer tolerate chaos and needed a peaceful environment. When the noise machine turned off, Sheri, relieved, relaxed more and slept longer.

Still, her decline continued.

Arizona!

For about a month, we had planned a trip to Arizona. Sheri wanted to make one last visit, before it got too late, to her high school classmate and lifelong friend Gale Ekiss in Mesa. At first, we planned to make a real trip of it, a visit to the Grand Canyon on the way to Phoenix and time in Sedona, one of the most spiritual places in Arizona. I even made reservations for the required hotels in early September although I wondered if Sheri could make it.

One day after I made the reservations, we talked. Her pain medication dosage continued to increase and she had little energy. It became clear the drive to Phoenix would be all she could endure.

We decided to cancel the hotels in the Grand Canyon and Sedona and drive straight to Phoenix in one day to minimize drive and motel time. The plan looked like it might come apart before we got started. We left in the morning September 15 and by the time we reached the outskirts of Corona, a half hour into the trip, Sheri needed to get a different pillow out the trunk because she felt tired and wanted to doze. We got off the freeway at Green River and when I reached to top of the exit I saw with horror traffic backed up across the bridge and on the freeway lanes toward Orange County.

I stopped and found the pillow, then we decided to drive through Corona to get back on the freeway because of all the traffic. It took an hour as we passed road after backed up road with all the paths to the freeway filled with cars. We stopped in

Corona to use the bathroom and get an iced tea, then resumed our safari across the car-strewn town of Corona. We found our way back onto the freeway in the south end of Riverside.

Sheri and Lee at Carol's birthday party Sept. 2, 2015

On the rest of this uneventful trip we drove through long stretches of desert and many miles with no facilities. We took every opportunity to use rest stops along the way but I knew she might have to go with no facilities in sight. We stopped in Blythe for lunch and then headed into Arizona. Sheri slept a lot along the way. She celebrated when we arrived in Phoenix about 5 p.m. and went straight to Gale's house. We ate dinner, talked, and went to bed early.

The next morning, all three of us drive up to the cabin near Payson, Arizona, where we planned to spend the next few days. At first, we had planned to take side trips but Sheri had no energy for them. Instead, she stayed at the cabin and spent her time with Gale while I took a few day trips.

First, I took a full day and drove to Sedona, a beautiful town in the red rock country. I stopped at Montezuma's Castle and the hillside mining town of Jerome. I had fun in Sedona, my first visit in many years. I went to two of the vortices Sedona is famous for (didn't feel any). Then as evening settled in, I headed up Oak Creek Canyon to Flagstaff and then returned the long way around to Payson, where I arrived a little after dark.

I also drove up to the lakes on top of the Mogollon Rim. This thousand-foot, hundred-mile-long cliff slices through the middle of Arizona. Along the way I stopped at a small area where you can find tiny fossils from millions of years ago.

Both Sheri and I relaxed, visited with Gale, played games and I completed a jigsaw puzzle. Sheri and Gale made Halloween cards by hand.

By this time, I knew we had taken our last road trip together although both of us looked forward to the holidays and the new year. We did take a drive up to the top of the Rim before we left the area but she could only manage about 20 miles or so. The trip home concerned me.

We both kept up a fiction: We faced little more than a hitch on the road to health and we still had months before us. I had no idea what the weeks after we got home would bring but I had this deep down, almost unconscious, sense they would include a steep decline. For now, she could walk and take care of herself and kept up her great attitude.

Then the time came for us to go home. On the way out of Phoenix Wednesday, September 23, we stopped at the lab to draw blood for a pre-chemo test before her next chemotherapy session, scheduled for the day after we got home. After the test, we made the long drive home. Sheri needed bathroom facilities more often these days so I made sure she knew about the distance to the next one as we drove out of Phoenix.

One of Sheri's beautiful cloud photos, Mogollon Rim, Arizona, Sept 2015

The next long stretch of desert had few facilities. She slept most of the time while I drove. We lunched in Blythe and arrived home early in the evening.

The Lull Before the Storm

Sheri did her chemo the day after we got back home, then we settled into the usual routine. At first, we went various places together and she worked in her garden. However, I noticed a dramatic increase in the amount of pain medication she took and noticed she ate less and less. She complained she had tightness in the abdomen area and filled up after a few bites. She took more liquid and less solid food and became very selective about what she ate.

The next Wednesday, when we walked to the car, she held onto my arm to steady herself.

The Fall

On Saturday, October 3, in the late afternoon, I left the house for a while. Before I returned home, I got a phone call from Sheri. She sounded scared when she told me she had fallen and believed she needed to get checked at the Urgent Care to make sure she hadn't injured herself. I would meet her at the facility since a friend offered to drive her.

Reality intervened. All the signs showed up, the continued weakness, increased medication, lack of food, and now the fall.

We waited for the Urgent Care to do tests. They came back negative. No strained muscles or broken bones, except her confidence. We went home.

By this time, she spent most of her time in her office, which she called the "Nest." In addition to the books and computer, she had a very comfortable bed which had pillows on the side she would use to support herself. Our bed didn't work because it required her to sleep on her back.

On Monday, she complained about burning in her esophagus and we decided to go to the emergency room for tests. She guessed she had a blockage in the abdomen area since she had a difficult time swallowing.

The doctors ordered a CAT scan and when it came back said they didn't see a problem in the esophagus but they noticed a swollen liver and bigger cancer lesions. Not good news. We asked the doctors to send the scan to Dr. Wagner since we planned to see him Wednesday, October 7.

The Oncologist Weighs In

I will never forget this meeting. All the thoughts and fears of the previous weeks flowed out. Sheri started out with, "I want to make sure we are on the same page here. I want a cure and I need you to be with me on this. Do you agree?"

Dr. Wagner thought for a moment, then said, "I can't. All along we could only give you as much time as possible. However, I want to continue the chemotherapy to see if it works." He added the CAT Scan was not conclusive and was not designed to tell if the cancer had progressed. They talked about the lack of appetite and Dr. Wagner scheduled an Upper GI for October 12 to see if a blockage would explain the pressure and lack of appetite.

He also asked if we had contacted Hospice yet. We both said no. He said he would send me a couple of names to check out.

I remember how much his words surprised Sheri and her subdued mood as we left. Her next chemo was scheduled for October 15, the next week. As we left, she held my arm and we took the elevator down instead of the stairs. She didn't say much on the way home.

I went out Thursday afternoon but when I returned home, I found a wheelchair in the living room. "I couldn't walk well," she said, "So I asked Maria (a neighbor) if she had one."

The next time we went out, the wheelchair accompanied us, folded up in the back seat while we drove. She ate less and less and got weaker. Sunday afternoon, we went to a play (Dracula) to support an actor friend of ours from Laguna Woods.

Time rushed along. Sheri got weaker by the day. She had more trouble with her medication and a very difficult time getting comfortable. She piled up pillows on the couch in the living room, moved then around, then around again.

Tuesday morning, we went back to Saddleback Hospital for the Upper GI. She felt uncomfortable as they prepared her and after they wheeled her out, I went home to await the results. After half an hour, they wheeled her back to the holding area and soon the doctor returned. He shook his head. "I didn't find problems in the abdomen area. The liver is swollen but all the organs work fine."

Most of us would take this as good news. Not us. If the organs worked, the problem existed elsewhere. The cancer. We asked the nurses to forward the results to Dr. Wagner for his opinion on where we went from here.

At home in the afternoon, she again struggled to get comfortable on the living room couch. I sensed her frustration. She couldn't find a workable position. I understood her great distress and could not help her.

About 5 Dr. Wagner called and we talked for about 15 minutes. He told me the cancer continued to grow faster and chemotherapy hadn't worked. I already guessed the truth. He suggested hospice. I asked how much time she might have left and he said three or four months, which surprised me.

I went back to the living room and told her what the doctor had said. After a brief discussion, she said, "Do you think it is time to call Hospice?" I said yes.

We enter Hospice

The dreaded word: Hospice. All treatment stops when this word is uttered. We have an image of gloomy, somber people who stand around in silence while the patent sleeps. Of course, this vision is ridiculous. Hospice workers are among the most caring in the world. They are available every minute of every day. They visit when needed. The do chores, bathe the patient, provide high-level equipment, provide all the medications you need for pain and discomfort, and act like a ray of fresh sunshine. We could all use a little hospice in our lives. On the other hand, it means the patient may not survive. As the end approaches, it looks more like a completion and a new beginning than a blank wall. The patient soon moves through a screen we cannot penetrate from this life to the same path we will all experience one day.

Wednesday morning, October 14, I called Saddleback Hospice, one of the organizations on our list. I selected them because of their association with the local hospital. They sent a nurse out about two o'clock to talk with us.

We listened and asked questions for about half an hour. The professionalism I saw and the services they would perform for us impressed me. We would have a nurse visit three times a week and could get all the equipment we needed.

Then Sheri said, "How soon can you have a hospital bed out here?"

"One hour," the nurse said.

"Do it." She signed the forms and we entered hospice. Within an hour., the adjustable bed arrived, along with an oxygen tank, a new commode, a package of emergency medications, and a new wheelchair.

She got into the bed and, except for a few steps to use the commode, never left it.

Lots of visitors

Caretaking can be a lonely task if the person you care for has few friends or is ill for a long time. After the novelty stops, most of the visitors stop as well. In the case of an acute illness, at first you get a few people who want to visit and a lot of calls. When the situation deteriorates, the flood of visitors grows until you need schedules and spreadsheets to deal with it. When the end approaches, everyone wants to show up at the same moment. It is best to limit visitors to close family and friends since visits task the strength of the patient and make the journey more difficult. They also provide energy and make the journey easier. When the balance is right, they give joy. I divide the groups into two, visitors and assistant caregivers. The visitors will chat, sit around, make noise, then leave. The assistant caretakers will sit in silence while the patient sleeps and will do what is needed to make her comfortable. Big difference.

Sheri spent a quiet first night in Hospice. My main problem concerned food and medications. She refused to take liquid medications so we stuck to pills. As the days passed, I gave her only the most important pills so she would not have to deal with so many of them.

Thursday, we sent out an email and messages to as many people as possible to tell them Sheri had entered Hospice. It came as no surprise to her close friends who had watched her grow weaker.

I took on the task to schedule visitors. We wanted to make sure people did not overburden her so I kept it down to one visitor at a time. The demand grew and the time slots remained limited. I made sure she had time to sleep and time to take care of personal matters.

On Friday, the Hospice aide gave her a bath and after she left scheduled visitors arrive one by one. We had at least five people visit.

Sheri and Pam, October 17, 2015 at home

Saturday, October 17, special visitors arrived. My sister Lynne had called a few days earlier to see if she and her husband could visit that day. Garry had attended a class reunion in Bakersfield and wanted to stop by before they went home. She also said that they did not plan to return to California for Thanksgiving or Christmas because of Garry's poor physical condition.

Lynne and Garry and my two nephews arrived about noon and we all went out to buy chicken and pumpkin pie for an afternoon feast. By this time, I knew Sheri would not eat much. However, she enjoyed the visit and I think all of us knew we would never again all be together as a family, the first of many sad goodbyes.

Over next few difficult days, I am glad most everyone had the opportunity to visit and make one last connection with Sheri.

The visits continued Sunday, Monday and Tuesday. Sheri's half-sister, who we had not seen in 20 years, came by as well as many friends and colleagues.

On Tuesday, we received a package of trust documents from our attorney. Sheri needed to sign them. I admit I thought we had weeks and even months of Hospice before Sheri might leave us. However, as the week wore on, it became evident she had lost strength faster than expected.

I asked Denise if she knew a traveling notary and she made the call. The notary arrived the afternoon of Thursday, October 22. When we started to sign the documents, it surprised me to see how much difficulty Sheri experienced as she attempted to write her name. We spent an excruciating hour or so with the documents and then the notary book.

This became a seminal moment for me. Her decline had accelerated. I knew about the weakness, the pills she could no longer swallow, the lack of food but to see this dramatic sign of change made a huge impression.

The rest of the week played out. More visitors came, we watched The Great Race and Colbert but she slept through most of it. On Sunday, October 25, her friend Jean came by and sang to her for a while.

On Monday, October 26, her high school friend Gale and another friend arrived for a visit from Arizona. We reserved the next day and a half for them. Tuesday night we had a small crisis. The bed didn't work right and made her very uncomfortable. She wanted to tell Hospice to replace the bed. We did replace the mattress but the bed still didn't work. When I went out to dinner, Gale called to ask me to search for a Memory Foam pad on the way home. I visited Kohl's and three Targets and got home about 9 p.m. with enough foam to fix the bed. She slept much easier.

Gale left about 11 a.m. Wednesday morning after a long goodbye. By this time, I could see Sheri's exhaustion and irritability. She ate little food and picked at what she did ask for. It came down to mango lasse with a small amount of protein powder.

In the evening, Denise Lamonte, Alice, Michelle Bogarin and Sherree Jolly hung out with Sheri while I worked in my office. Denise came in and said Sheri wanted to meet with all of us.

We gathered around the bed. "I am exhausted," Sheri said. "All the visitors create too much noise and confusion and I need it to stop."

"Do you want to cancel the visitors? We have several scheduled," I said.

"No more visitors," she said. "I am ready to die and I don't want any more people here." She looked at Alice. "I want you to be with me through the rest of this. I need the chaos to end."

I canceled all visitors.

It didn't go over well. People who wanted to see her did not get to do so. It couldn't be helped.

Alice, Sherree, Denise, and Michelle became the core group who stayed with her most of the rest of the way.

In the afternoon, we purchased a baby monitor so I could hear Sheri if she needed help at night. I had assisted her more and more when she needed to use the commode but she had managed at night. Thursday night, she woke me up about two o'clock in the morning for help. It went okay but disturbed sleep is not good and I spent the next day tired.

Friday morning, her Mastermind Group held their meeting at the house from 10:30 to 11:30. Sheri slept most of the day but again woke me up at 2 a.m. This time she wanted a nurse to come to the house. I waited up until five before she arrived and went to bed exhausted. When I got up later Saturday, Sheri had called Denise and asked her to stay overnight with her. The next afternoon, Pam and Yvette visited and stayed until 5 p.m. while the rest of us left them alone.

As we sat in the living room just before they left, Sheri looked around and asked, "Do you see all the people here?"

I said, "Just us."

"No," she said. "I see are a lot of people in the room, both of alive and dead." She pointed to the arm of the couch. "My guide is on the edge of the sofa. He looks like a 17-year-old boy."

Then she napped.

Denise arrived in the late afternoon and stayed with Sheri Saturday night, October 31.

THREE

Financial Disaster and Recovery December 2008 to December 2013

Brilliant Decisions

Over the next three years, Sheri and I made three brilliant decisions. They didn't feel brilliant at the time but turned out to be critical our subsequent financial success.

As you read this section, be aware we planned none of this. We faced horrible financial problems, had no money, lived on credit cards, faced a looming house payment increase and credit limits on the cards. I am amazed the card companies let us run up this much debt in such a bad economy. No new cards or increased credit lines but excellent credit played a role.

First Brilliant Decision

A friend we had met at one of the Speak Your Way to Wealth events had gone into the insurance business. In 2010, I did not want to spend more money on insurance but he sat us down in his office and went over where we stood and suggested we get a new life insurance policy on each of us. Sheri had about $70,000 and I had a small policy of $15,000. He suggested we get higher limits and pointed out the new policies had an acceleration clause. It would pay off if either of us got sick, either chronic or fatal, within six months. I didn't qualify because a test came back too far off average. It later turned out to be no problem.

However, Sheri passed her tests and we got a life insurance policy for $135,000 with a premium of $75 a month. We had no idea at the time we would need it. We were both healthy, age 62 and 65. What could happen?

Second Brilliant Decision

As I mentioned earlier, my sister and I owned my mother's house in Placentia and rented it to the assistant minister at the church. In October 2010, he informed us the church wanted him to move into a house it owned and he needed to end our rental agreement.

Lynne and I took one look at the house and decided we had only one alternative, sell it for as much as we could get. Real estate prices had increased over the past year so we could get a competitive price, although not as good as we could have gotten in 2008. We couldn't rent it out because my mother had neglected the house for years and neither of us had enough money to do the needed repairs.

We hired an agent and after a lengthy process, found a buyer. We had to share repair expenses with the buyer, which included termite repairs, new windows, structural work, and tenting. Escrow closed in July 2011. When the dust settled

Lynne and I each had about $135,000 in the bank. Again, we didn't plan this brilliant decision. It only became brilliant two years later when the drama unfolded. I believe a lot of such brilliant decisions are wonderful in retrospect, but not so good at the time. What could be wrong with money in the bank?

At first, this came as a relief but I also realized we owed $200,000 on credit cards, a mortgage $250,000 more than the value of our house, and the house payment would go from $1900 a month to over $5,000 a month in November. The numbers didn't add up at all.

Now we knew why we couldn't have cash in the bank while we owed a fortune to creditors. If we declare bankruptcy, the $135,000 goes in a flash, along with the only place we had to live. What a problem! We had no idea how important an asset the cash would become.

Third Brilliant Decision

Bankrupt. No question about it. No way to pay our debts. But, we had the pesky $135,000 in the bank.

We shopped bankruptcy attorneys. Most of them wanted us fill out a form and file right then. They didn't ask about our specific needs.

We talked to the fourth one because a local publication rated her as one of the best attorneys in Orange County. When we sat down with her, she listened, then told us the money could be a problem and we should not file for bankruptcy. She mentioned lookbacks, etc. and said we had to wait a while before we filed.

Meanwhile, we needed to short sell our house, which brought up the problem of where to live. She also said we needed to invest the cash. Real estate would be best place. Our first thought: "It's Orange County, California, it's expensive here. And in our financial condition we'll never qualify for a loan."

We looked around. All the properties were priced way beyond our price range. Then a friend suggested Laguna Woods, south of Irvine. We found a few units priced under $50,000 and many others in our price range.

We searched for a month in late 2011 and found and made an offer on a perfect two-bedroom unit with a patio converted to a room. We got it for $109,900, paid cash, and had enough left over to rebuild the kitchen. We moved to our new home in January 2012.

The Irvine house took longer to sell but closed at the last minute in June 2012. All the stuff went into two storage units and we settled in.

Speak Your Way to Wealth

About this time, Arvee and I decided to stop Speak Your Way to Wealth since the recession had changed the parameters and people no longer spent as much as before 2008.

We decided to concentrate on our own programs. About this time, I started the CSL Writers Workshop with Dr. Jim Turrell and Arvee centered her speaker training on the Christian market.

We Face the Music

The payment on the house went up in November 2011. Our cash flow could not cover all the bills. Our lawyer advised us to stop mortgage and the credit card payments. She said it would take a long time for them to come after us and we needed to do this for at least a year.

We followed her instructions. To my surprise, we had a few months of notices and a few phone calls but we wrote a letter to each creditor and told them to stop contact with us, which they did. The silence amazed me. Toward the end of 2012, we got a few lawsuits and I made a few court appearances.

We checked with the attorney, who agreed we could go ahead with the bankruptcy so in early 2013 we filed and completed the case by July. In the end, we had no debts, a paid for house, a new car, and a new life.

The whole experience brought Sheri and I closer together as we settled into our new life.

We move in early 2012

Unless you have experienced it, you have no idea of the peace that descended on our household the day in late January when we moved into our new home in Laguna Woods.

As I mentioned earlier, we had purchased the house in October and since we still had the Irvine house we had no rush to move.

I spent a lot of time in Laguna Woods as I tore out the entire kitchen down to the cement floor and removed several closets inside the front door so we would have an open-style kitchen and living room.

Sheri and I spent a lot of time at Home Depot on the design of our new kitchen. She enjoyed every minute of it since she loved design and this gave her a chance to make the new house hers. This move downsized us from a 1,750-square-foot house with a two-car garage to a 1,200-square-foot house with a carport. A lot of stuff had to go, either out the door in a garage sale or into a storage unit.

I had several months to sort out the garage but when garage sale time came in the Spring of 2012, we still had a huge amount of stuff at the house. We must have sold a thousand dollars' worth of stuff to the hundreds of people who came by. We had stuff in the living room, the kitchen, the foyer, the patio and the garage, thousands of items from my past, Sheri's past and from my parents' past. We had shelf after shelf of tools, furniture, knickknacks, clothes, and miscellany.

I recommend downsizing to get rid of accumulated stuff (notice I didn't call it junk) in an organized manner. Even years later, I still have more than I need in the storage units but I will handle it.

After January, we settled in and began to explore the many services and organizations Laguna Woods offered. Sheri discovered dance classes and movie programs, joined the Bocce Club, and we joined the Baby Boomers Club for the dances. Our lifestyle shifted. We could relax, stop the worry about money and get back to building our businesses.

Manchitas

Our wonderful dog Manchitas accompanied us to the new house. By now she was 14 years old and for the past year had shown signs of age. She could no longer jump up on the bed and fell down a few times. In February, we noticed she threw up more and more. She lost energy fast. The vet said it might be cancer. He couldn't isolate it without a bunch of expensive tests.

After a few weeks, she couldn't keep food down, she had no energy and she faded fast. In the Spring of 2012, we made one final visit to the vet to say goodbye to her and to put her to sleep, a sad moment for both us. Manchitas was a gentle, loving dog whose spirit would never leave us. She brought us joy, she traveled with us, sleeping in the back seat on long drives, never complained, and took every turn in stride.

Sally Arrives

I didn't want to get another dog. We loved Manchitas but we also had three cats in a much smaller house. Manchitas did not fit well into our new house, okay now but a problem in her younger years, when she loved to race up the stairs and roam the front patio.

However, Sheri missed her dog because she had dogs as a child. These constant loving companions never hassled her like her parents did. They became a source of comfort for her and she felt lost without one.

We visited the Irvine Animal Shelter July 2012 and after we looked at a few dogs, we found a six-year-old Jack Russell with a reasonable personality and adopted her. We named her Sally. This active little pup became an immediate hit in the neighborhood with her upbeat personality and ecstatic greeting of everyone she met.

Sheri wants out of her job

By this time, Sheri had tired of her job counseling victims of crime, most of them children. It depressed her and consumed a lot of her energy. Most of the children came from Hispanic families since she spoke fluent Spanish and many came from broken homes with at least one absent parent. It paid well but took a huge toll on her.

I can't say I blame her for wanting out of her job. I heard too many sad stories of kids broken before they got out of high school. I felt her pain and exhaustion at the long hours she listened to them and now I understand her stress even more as I learn more about her own rough childhood.

In the summer of 2013, she contacted companies to begin to rebuild her consulting and training business. She looked forward to helping managers and employees work together.

Not much happened for quite a few months so she plugged away at the counseling job and the few individual clients she had left. She also had a lot of meetings. When I go through all the files from late 2013 I see lots of discussions and proposals. They went nowhere. I know the lack of results frustrated her.

Sheri Writes Her Book

Early in 2013, after we got settled into our new house, Sheri decided she wanted to write a book to help her get consulting clients. She wanted to show managers how to work with their Hispanic workforces. She wrote very powerful stories about her days in Mexico and had picked out photos to use. Still, the project lagged.

We start the Writers Workshop

At the 2013 annual meeting of the Center for Spiritual Living our minister Jim Turrell happened to mention he thought he might want to set up a writers group for members of the church. He had written several books and suggested I, seated in the back of the room, might want to be part of it.

After the meeting, I said, "Let's talk more about this." It went from concept to full-fledged idea very fast. By April we planned a live event, in May we reserved a room at National University, and on June 21, 2013, we held the first session of the

CSL Writers Workshop with 20 eager writers in the audience. Sheri joined us. We met once a month for three months and by the end of the three sessions, Sheri had a rough draft ready to go.

The Workshop has grown and changed in the past three years into a powerful online program. I can see it take off and bring in a lot of money. I am sad Sheri did not live to see the dream mature.

She wrote her book, *How to Manage Your Hispanic Workforce*, though. Over the rest of the year she spent a lot of time on it. By Christmas she had it ready for an edit. Since she had a resident editor at home, the book came together fast and we published it on Kindle March 17, 2014.

The Fourth Brilliant Decision

On March 31, 2013, Sheri turned 65 and became eligible for Medicare. She was off insurance for several months after a run of expensive temporary polices. With great relief, she signed up for Medicare.

At the time, she went to a holistic doctor in Irvine who took Medicare only with a PPO plan. I had never used my Medicare plan in three years so we signed up for what she needed.

Our Blue Cross plan had an 80-20 pay plan and we paid the deductibles and co-pays without supplemental insurance. After all, why would a healthy couple pay hundreds of dollars a month when we saw no prospect of serious illness. It worked for us at the time.

By the late 2013, she stopped seeing the holistic doctor and when open enrollment period arrived, we discussed a new insurance plan. We called on the expertise of one of Sheri's friends, a Medicare specialist. We wanted to keep expenses to a minimum since we still faced a tight financial position even though the bankruptcy took care of our major debts. Income still presented a problem.

Our specialist pointed out our two real choices, take regular Medicare and buy a supplemental insurance policy for copays or join a Medicare Advantage plan. The supplemental policy would cost a few hundred a month we didn't have. The advantage plan had no premium, no co-pay for doctors, specialists, or hospitals and $65 for an emergency room visit if the doctors did not admit her to the hospital.

We made the easy decision and on January 1, 2014, our new insurance policy with SCAN took effect. What an inspired decision!

All looks well

We welcomed in the new year with all our problems behind us. We had financial security, Sheri's business readied for takeoff, mine took giant steps, we had great insurance, lived in a great community, and had a wonderful group of close friends. When New Year's Day 2014 dawned, we slept in, then watched part of the Rose Parade, and took an easy day for ourselves. On this sunny day with a high near 70 degrees, Sheri's optimism boiled over at the prospect of the bright future that awaited us. With her book out and clients on the horizon, she looked forward to her best ever new year.

Part VII

2015

Saturday,
The Seventh Day in November

ANGER

I'm angry at fleas. Or at least, I was today when they presented a major obstacle to my following thru with my well laid plans for the day. I had to cancel a foot massage appointment. I got totally befuddled and confused when problem was presented and it appeared today was the best day to handle it. I hate being out of control. It also made me mad that it was going to cost a small fortune to do it right this time. You know what it did? It got me off my butt. I had been sitting around commiserating, feeling sorry for myself when what I need to realize is I have everything I need right now. Right now, I'm OK. I have resources, outlets, answers. They may not be what I think I want right now but it's what I've got today and that's where it's at. When I get back to practicing, or observing, my spiritual program, I know that what I'm supposed to have in order to learn my lessons. Back to anger. It's a bitch. I'm angry I can't have everything I want. I need to get to know me. But can't I have a good time in the meantime? I want to be free, not hampered by other opinions. What they think of me is none of my business. She'll survive. That's life. Why not allow myself the nurturing now? And keep myself spread thin with other friends so I don't get totally confused. "Totally" doesn't ring true. I can control it. Ha, ha, ha. Who cares. Go 4 it!!

Sheri Long

August 29, 1986

ONE

She Is Still Here,
Saturday, November 7, 2015

We all awoke about seven Saturday morning to find Sheri had not slipped away the night before. She stayed very much present and in about the same unconscious but anxious state which had persisted for much of the week.

"What are we still missing?" I asked. The more I worked to uncover it, the more the missing problem stayed out of reach by my consciousness. Her parents and family were the problem. We gave her the solution. Or did we?

"Did you ever hear from Paco, her Mexican godson?" Sherree asked.

"No," I said. Then it clicked in my mind. Five or six years before, Sheri injured one of his puppies while she played with it. The dog recovered but Paco stayed angry and for years would not talk to her. Could this be the problem?

I went to Sheri's computer and found the email addresses for both Paco and his aunt Rocio, one of Sheri's best friends in

Mexico, and sent off a note about Sheri at 7:15 a.m. I hoped he would get it and answer soon.

At eight the LVN nurse, who had worked the previous evening, returned for the day shift. We welcomed her back and updated her on overnight events.

Diane from across the walk stopped by about 9:30 a.m. We asked if she saw anyone on the porch the previous night but she said no, she didn't get up then.

When Diane left, Sherree and Alice and I went to breakfast at Starbucks and talked about the situation.

It may be odd but, while most people wait in silence for the inevitable passing, we took an active role to figure out what we needed to do to make the passing she wanted so much happen.

When we returned at 11, I went to my computer to check the email. Paco had answered about an hour earlier. His short email said, "Dear Lee, this is Paco, this notice makes me deeply sad, Sheri always be for me my mom, I don't have words to explain the pain in my heart. I don't know what to do. I wish say to Sheri I love her."

At 11:30 I read the email to Sheri and Alice called out from the kitchen, "Wow, I felt a wave of joyous energy sweep through the kitchen!"

Sherree and Alice and I gathered in the kitchen.

"This might be what we needed," Alice said. She thanked Sherree for remembering them. "I hope Sheri can leave now," she said.

We decided we should act normal and see what happened in the afternoon. I went to lunch and returned about 1:30. I had a strange lunch, laced with a mixture of anticipation and foreboding. I still had no idea what I would feel in the moment

Sheri passed, whenever such time might arrive. Yet I wanted her to pass from this life in peace.

When I got home, Sheri appeared to be in much the same state as before. The Shaman called Alice again. After an update, she told Alice to call in the "ancestors", who would include spiritual guides and actual ancestors of Sheri's. These would be the spirits she would be closest to. "They may be able to help her over the obstacles she faces," she said. Alice agreed and put out the call.

Sheri's friend Michelle Bogarin arrived about 4:30 p.m. Around then, Sheri opened her eyes and attempted to speak to Michelle but nobody could understand her.

We sat around the table to discuss our next move. Alice thought we needed to do one final journey to rebuild the wounded relationships with Paco and Rocio. I agreed, given her argument with Paco. By then I had no idea what still needed to happen to bring peace to Sheri. We decided to do it but decided to eat dinner before we embarked on this journey, which we hoped would be the last.

We ordered Thai food from Elephant Thai and had it delivered.

Before we ate, Alice took all of us through an exercise to plant us in this reality before we stepped into the edge of the next one. She then called in the eight sentinels to guard Sheri again. They gathered at the four points of the bed and stood watch while we ate.

We ate a strange dinner, like the last supper before a momentous event took place. As I think back on it, we made more careful preparations for this journey than we had the last, undertaken in haste and urgency. This one would cure a minor glitch with one long-time relationship but we sensed our journey had a greater importance. We didn't know why.

We put away the food and prepared in silence. This time each of us held a white rose and Sherree and Alice again connected themselves with the red ribbon.

Alice said, "Be sure to stay on the first level of the matrix this time. The second level can be very dangerous since you might get caught in Sheri's web of relationships and not be able to get back."

This time, Sheri would go to the second platform alone.

Again, we met Sheri in the contact place Alice had set up. Alice explained the steps and again Sheri consented. We emerged from her place, crossed the river and went across the plain to a huge structure. To me it looked like wooden scaffolding with two flat platforms with a wooden floor. A railing surrounded the platform. In the distance, I could see more platforms.

We again climb the stairs and Sherree and I stop on the first level and observe from below. I look up and feel like I jump up and down between the two platforms. I can see the third platform in the distance as a sea of sharp black plates shifting like stiff waves. I stay on the first but my vision wants to see the second. It does look dangerous and hard to pin down.

Sheri walks up to the second platform and again addresses two spirits but we cannot see who they are. She cuts the cord with one and keeps the cord with the other. I assume she kept the tie with Paco but we cannot be sure. With the ceremony complete, we leave the first platform and go down the stairs. As the four of us reach the bottom of the stairs, her stepfather joins us. We cross the plain back to Sheri's interim home.

As we approach the bridge over the river that heads to her bed, we see a crowd of souls in front of us, waiting for us to cross the bridge.

Alice says these are the ancestors she called in to help us. We approach the bridge, Harold beside Sheri and the rest of us behind. A woman steps forward from the crowd, carrying a small bundle with care, as if it held a great treasure.

We cross the bridge over the river. We hear the ancestors call the bundle "The Gift." At first, Sheri is curious but Alice notices her become more agitated as we walk.

Then we all stop. We are close now and Alice notices the bundle is a child. "I had no idea what that meant," she said later. "I thought the child came from one of the ancestors who gave it to Sheri to comfort her."

Sheri stops when sees the child. She holds up her hands in horror as if she wards off an evil spirit. "No. No No. Take it away," she says.

The ancestors hold the child out. Alice still does not understand what it means. She is surprised at Sheri's reaction, as it is all out of proportion to the event.

Sheri backs away from the bundle. Harold takes her hand and stops her. "It is a gift," he says. "Take it." Sheri calms down and with reluctance accepts the child. She holds it away from her at first, then I see silent words pass between them, a serious communication about an event known only to the two of them.

After a few moments, she draws the child in closer, then hugs it to her breast. While the rest of us and all the ancestors wait in quiet, Sheri walks a short distance to the bed, curls up on it with the child cuddled in her arms and goes to sleep.

It is about 7 p.m. We are seated in the living room near Sheri's bed. Everyone is in tears. Alice talks about the gift, still with no idea what it meant.

I said, "I know who the child is."

Alice said, "I guessed the child came from one of the ancestors. Who is it?'

I took a deep breath. "Back when Sheri was 22, in 1970, she got pregnant and had an abortion. You know she never liked children and didn't want them."

"The child was hers!" Alice broke in tears. "Her child!" We broke into tears now.

I asked, "Did Sheri ever tell you about the abortion?"

"No, never," Alice said. "I had no idea."

The child belonged to Sheri and she had not allowed it to live here on earth. I believe she must have repressed it so deep she wanted to believe no consciousness followed death and therefore this event of years ago would not follow her. It explained her deep reluctance to cross over to the other side where she might have to face the child (and face her mother as well) and the consequences once she discovered death would not save her. The ancestors gave her the gift of forgiveness and the gift of the child from so many years ago who waited for her to arrive so she could be a true mother to it.

We sat in silence as we absorbed this lesson and knew this might be the final piece of the puzzle. A sense of peace came over the room, unlike what I had felt since this drama began a week earlier. Sheri rested in comfort. We could do no more.

The afternoon nurse left about 8 and the night nurse arrived. Sheri had a fever so we put cold packs around her to lower the fever.

About nine, Michelle left. She told me later she went to her car, checked both ways and saw no traffic. She got in the car and looked in the rear vision mirror. A coyote sat in the middle of the road and stared at her car. After a few minutes, he left. Michelle looked this up and found the coyote is considered a trickster and a playful creature, like Sheri. A message??

The night charge nurse arrived about 10:30. At first, she acted like all the other nurses. With a businesslike professionalism, she went about her job. In my first impression, she looked stern, all business, and said little. We think we might want this in a nurse with important medical decisions to make.

After she left, we noticed she had not reset one of the pain medicine meters for the night and called her to come back. She arrived about midnight.

After she took care of the morphine drip, she looked around the room and noticed the aromatherapy vials scattered about.

In a sudden instant, her entire demeanor changed. She said, "Wait a minute." She went to her car and returned a few minutes later with a package of various aromatherapy items, and pulled out an orange oil. She said, "This is very special."

The she said, "I'm taking off my nurse hat and putting on my intuitive hat." She said she seldom let people see this part of her. She sat beside the bed and held Sheri's hand in silence for half an hour. The rest of also sat in silence with her. She said a few words I didn't hear, then added, "It is better to let Sheri rest in peace for now and let her adjust to her new reality. Don't do any more journeys. She will pass when she is ready, tomorrow or Monday."

Then she said, "All the Canadian and United States Indian Nations are drumming for Sheri, even the Blackfeet, who often don't." Then she increased the morphine dose again and said, "Don't give her any more extra amounts."

About 1 a.m. she left and all of us went to bed.

Part VIII

2015

Sunday,

The Eighth Day in November

ONE

Resting and Decline
Sunday, November 8, 2015

I awoke at 7 a.m. to a scene of confusion and distress. The night nurse had continued to give Sheri extra doses of morphine during the night and the system had run dry about 6 a.m. Sheri was in distress. It took hours to get a new bag ordered and delivered. Once the nurse installed the new bag, the morphine drip resumed, Sheri calmed down again, breathing in measured breaths followed by silent intervals.

The morning nurse arrived about eight and after discussion with her, Sherree noticed she wore a Mickey Mouse watch on her wrist. We glanced at each other. Then came the silent agreement. Sheri's gift to me Friday night. What else could we expect under the circumstances.

We hung around for a while. I went into my office to work and about 11:30 went to lunch.

When I got back, the nurses said they needed to work with Sheri in private. She bruised herself from laying in the same place for many hours and they wanted to move her but wanted us to leave because she might experience pain, which made sense to me. They told us return in a few hours.

Sherree and Alice and I went to Starbucks and sat in the patio in the sun to reminisce about the day's events and figure out why Sheri didn't leave.

About 2 p.m. Denise Lamonte came by the house to visit but the nurses would not let her in. She called me and left a message and I called her back a few minutes later and invited her to come over to Starbucks and join us.

For the first time, I told her the entire story of the last week from beginning to end.

About 4:30 we head back to the house and find Sheri breathing with 15- to 45-second intervals between breaths. We think this is a sign she might go soon and sit with her one after the other. However, she keeps breathing the same way with no change.

About five, Sheri's friend Jean Turrell calls and sings beautiful songs to Sheri over the phone. She keeps breathing in the same way so we decide to keep to our normal activities and let her be.

Later, about 10 p.m., the night nurse came by again and checked Sheri, who still breathed with long stretches in between. Lorraine sits with us in silence for half-an-hour, then leaves. We had no more to say.

Or did we?

Part IX

2015
Monday,
The Ninth Day in November

Creative Intelligence abounds in everyone. We are always part of it. We dip into the creative juices and create beauty, when we connect consciously with spirit. My intention is to stay consciously connected all the time. I observe my demonstrations to stay aware of my divine connection. I'm grateful to know that I'm always living hand in hand with spirit, moment-to-moment all day. I let go of struggle to connect because it's already a done deal. So 'tis.

Sheri Long
August 22, 2015

ONE

The Beginning
Part 2
Monday, November 9, 2015

When I got up at 7 a.m. and went into the living room, Alice and Sherree stood around Sheri. She took light breaths with long gaps in between. Alice says she senses Sheri is a long way away by now but still she lingers. What keeps her here?

Sherree remembered she had wanted to hear what her friends might say at her memorial. We had planned to have friends come by November 1 for a living memorial but had to cancel it. Instead we asked people to send her tributes by email.

"We have a lot of emails of these," I said. "Why don't I make a file of them?"

Sherree agreed so I went into my office and took about half-an-hour to consolidate them into one file and send them to Alice's phone. I put one about Sally and her new home in the file too.

The document ended up 15 pages long. I liked the one about Sally, our Jack Russell dog who we had to give up in September because it told us how Sally had found a new, loving home on the beach in Newport Beach, which would make Sheri happy. I took a shower while Sherree read them to Sheri.

At 8 a.m., I got a call from our next LVN. He could not find the house. I went out and guided him in. By the time he arrived, Sheri experienced more fever and we added cold packs to get her temperature down and give her more comfort. We had to bring him up to date on Sheri's condition.

At 9:30 a.m., all three of us stand in the living room around Sheri's bed. She is quiet and we reminisce about her and about the week we have experienced. Her breathing is light now and peaceful.

Then I noticed she has not breathed in a while. At the same moment, I hear the front door open and Susan Leone walks in and rushes to Sheri's bedside. She holds Sheri's hand in silence. We all notice Sheri no longer breathes. She has made her decision. She has completed her life in this world and embarks on the next journey the moment her best friend arrives to be with her.

And Life Goes On

A few minutes after the nurse declared Sheri had passed at 9:50 a.m., David Sullenger called and I told him what had happened.

Our wonderful RN arrived at 10, already aware of Sheri's passing since the LVN had let her know. We removed all the cold packs from around Sheri and placed a blanket over her with her face uncovered. She looks relaxed and at peace with the world after her week of struggle. The RN had the LVN call the Cremation Society. We gave her the last of the pills and she put them in a diaper to dispose of them. A few spilled onto the floor so we had to clean them up. After a while the black table the nurses had used is clear, all the materials are sorted and packed up and removed and she hugs us all and leaves.

Joy arrived about 10:30 a.m. and helped comfort me when Alice and Sherree, exhausted by the drama of the past week, said they needed to go home to go to bed and sleep.

Smart Cremation arrived about 11, all dressed in black and suitably somber. With respectful care, they prepared Sheri to be removed from the living room.

After they left, Joy and I talked for a while and then she took all the rest of the diapers we had left over to the laundry room in case others in our complex wanted them. This informal Laguna Woods redistribution system gave items we didn't need to others who could use them. Very efficient.

Joy left about one and I closed the house and went to Panera for lunch about two. Both David Hartl and Michael Moon called me at lunch and I told them what had happened. I returned home about 2:45 and started to put loose items away while I waited for Hospice to come and collect the rest of their equipment, including the bed.

At 4:15 hospice came and took away the bed, oxygen tank, cords, the commode and the wheelchair. After they closed the door and left, I sat on the couch for a while in the living room and stared at the carpet, wrinkled up and covered with bits of litter. The emergence of the cats and a bit of purring broke the sudden silence.

The journey ended, all of it, all the waiting, all the fear, all the pain and all the foreboding. In its wake, Sheri's passing left joy and sadness, left hope for the future and an empty spot so big I at first had no idea how to fill it. All the noise, all of the effort and caring, vanished into thin air, leaving an empty physical reality behind. My dear wife of 22 years left long before her time. The void she left in my life would take a long time to fill, if ever.

Around me I saw an empty room with a void that replaced her bed, a carpet wrinkled by constant foot traffic, chairs and table in the wrong places, and bits of debris scattered everywhere.

I saw one obvious first step. Clean up the room. I straightened the rug, moved the furniture into place, vacuumed the rug as if on autopilot and put clothes in the washing machine. Then I sat and observed. The room looked perfect, every detail in place, like a museum, but with the life that used to animate it gone.

Bob Estrada called and I told him the story of Sheri and her journey. It helped my mood. While we talked, I folded items from the clothes dryer.

At 8 p.m., I watched *Dancing With the Stars*. Sheri loved the show. She enjoyed every dance and now, near the end of the season, the dancers still on the show put on incredible performances. I felt her watch it with me which gave me a lot of comfort.

After the show ended at 10:30 p.m., Michelle Bogarin called and told me the me the coyote story I shared in the chapter on Saturday.

A bit later, Joy called to invite me to dinner with her and Jerry Tuesday evening. I accepted. Then I went to bed.

Part X

2015

Tuesday,
After the Ninth Day in November

The pilgrim stands at the gates of forever. The pathless beauty stretches away to unknowable mountain fastnesses.

What happens when we walk through this timeless expanse, where no boundaries exist, no path leads, and each flower calls with a breathless, silent voice, "Come to me, join me, be one with me."?

The pilgrim has no way to choose options. Every step leads in the same direction, to beauty, to color, to welcome. The rainbow that marks a way forward brightens across the sky, a boundary she can never reach.

Where is she? Is this the edge of life, the beginning or the end, or is it even possible to tell?

We know not what is real or imagination. Both look the same. We know not where the first step will take us.

The pilgrim stands. Life lies behind and life lies ahead. Is it of the Earth or of some other place? She sees beauty, love and caring. She sees wonder and majesty.
She steps forward.

Lee Pound
November 11, 2016

The Legacy of a Lifetime

Sheri's life came down to nine days of waiting, nine days in which with her last flicker of life, she set her legacy in no uncertain terms. All else amounted to preparation.

She could have gone in silence, as so many do, leaving their survivors wondering. Instead she chose to go out with a message to the world: What we do matters, what we repress makes a difference, and who we forgive defines us forever. She did it without a word.

She didn't want to linger and yet linger she did until we got the message.

As I write this, I am at Lucille's Barbecue for dinner two days before New Year's 2016. I spent much of the difficult last month and a half inside and wrote very little. I knew it mattered but my mind held me back. I couldn't go deep enough yet. I couldn't let it all out. Too difficult. To move a finger felt like a thousand-pound weight. When I let them, the words came, flowed even, then tapered as if I had released too much energy.

Last night, as I drifted off to sleep, for the first time in a month I sensed Sheri beside me wearing the red coat I gave her for Christmas and could hear her words in my head for the first time ever. I couldn't make out or remember the words but with the communication came a sense of joy and discovery I couldn't generate in myself.

Earlier today I opened a box and found a file from the seventies and eighties of the last century. She had her own business, attended Toastmasters and had begun her mission in life with speeches outside the club on important subjects like alcoholism recovery.

This broadened my picture of her before we met and showed her strength even in those early days.

I sit here in Lucille's Barbecue a few days before the new year begins and it is clear she urges me forward. "You know the message! You have thought about it for years. Only you can hold yourself back."

I hear her words, not said in life but voiced from beyond and know she is right.

Three Months of Recovery

Even as I write this in June 2016, I am still in recovery. The first three months, before the Memorial, are a blur.

A week after she passed, I found a couple of Science of Mind magazines from October and November in a vertical file in her office "Nest." She last used the room October 13. I picked them up and took them into my office. A few days later I picked one up and noticed a bookmark in it. The November issue. When I opened it to the bookmarked page and saw the date, November 9, the day she passed, I felt a shiver of recognition.

A week later, I woke up one morning to find a vision of her seated beside me on the edge of the bed dressed in the bright red coat I had given her for Christmas. No words and a big smile. The vision lasted a few minutes before she faded away again.

Thanksgiving I spent with my nephews at their step-mother's house in Moorpark, California.

By December I began to clean out Sheri's office and looked for her boxes of memories as I started work on this book in earnest.

Three friends invited me to three Christmas dinners. I made it to all three. Such good friends and such good hospitality.

Bob Estrada, a great friend and solid rock of support through this journey, distracted me with a high-speed Ferrari run in 2015 to lunches at Brio and gatherings with his Ferrari friends. He and his wife Diane went through a cancer scare a few years before Sheri became ill. Diane beat hers and became an inspiration for Sheri in her days of need. One day in March or April, when I attended church, Bob came over and said, "Hey, tell Sheri to stop waking me up at night and telling me to call you!" Just like Sheri, I thought.

Sherree Jolly, another wonderful friend, stood by me through Sheri's illness and invited me to a tour of the Jet Propulsion Laboratory, and dinner on the beach in Huntington Beach, and a private tour of Griffith Park Observatory with her and her new boyfriend as I worked to recover from Sheri's passing. She also helped me clear out Sheri's clothes (very difficult – I put it off quite a while) and got them to a charity Sheri would like.

I have reconnected with most of the friends who helped in Sheri's last days. I can't say enough about their dedication and selfless energy when called upon to serve.

Writing this book is a labor of love. I went through the storage units and found box after box filled with memories of Sheri's past.

She kept photo albums, pictures, business materials, and best of all, writings she dated and filed, as if she knew I would need these items to tell her story one day.

As I read through and sorted all this information into boxes, I came to appreciate even more the woman she started out as and the woman she became. Her life inspired so many people. It is my privilege to share a small portion of it with you through this book.

If her story makes even a small difference in your life, all the joy, sorrow, and pain is worth it.

And yes, I am at work on the print version of her book, *How to Manage Your Hispanic Workforce.*

A Final Farewell

A few days before she went unconscious, Sheri gave us strict orders on what had to be in her memorial service. Because of the holidays and my six days in San Diego in January, we set the date for Sunday, January 31.

I don't know if Sheri had a hand in it but the day turned out to be one of worst weather days of Winter. Between wind, crashing waves and flooding, I applauded the miracle that most of our guests even arrived. One friend got blown off the freeway and had to return home. Pam and Yvette, her step-sister and friend-sister, had not arrived by the start time so I called them. They had just turned onto Michelson Drive, a few minutes away. Pam had driven all the way from Santa Barbara in this mess.

Most everyone wore red, her favorite color, as she had ordered. We called it a celebration of her life, not a memorial, and played upbeat music.

The crowd built and built until about 150 people crowded the room. I looked across this expanse of red and other colors and at the faces, all in celebration mode.

Our minister, Jim Turrell, said a few words then turned the show over to me. Pam went first with hilarious stories of her childhood with Sheri. The audience couldn't stop laughing. Sherree Jolly shared tales of Sheri's last 20 years. And Carol Rawe, Susan Leone, and David Hartl talked about personal and professional years.

To finish the eulogies, I told several stories from our marriage, many of which are included in this book. As I talked, I marveled at the spots we had gotten ourselves in and how we had handled them with humor and positivity.

Then Jeffrey Briar, the leader of the Laguna Laughter Club, led the audience in a Laughter Yoga exercise. In case you don't know, Laughter Yoga is laughter for no reason because laughter is one of the most therapeutic actions you can take. The audience stood up and participated with gusto.

Daniel Tyler-Pohnke, from our Frontier Trainings group, sang a beautiful song and then we wrapped it up with the Macarena.

The what? You might ask. You saw right. The Macarena. Sheri lived to dance and ordered us more than once to include it. Everyone had a blast and then filed into the social hall for a wonderful potluck and remembrance.

I felt Sheri's presence in the room at the celebration and know she inspired the words I said. I planned none of them but I am certain she guided me as I talked. I felt completion. We had given Sheri a monumental completion to her life in November. Now, in January, we gave her a sendoff into her new future she could be proud of.

At the reception, Alice took me aside and said, "While we did Laughter Yoga, I felt Sheri sneak into my head."

"And?" I asked.

"She looked around the room," Alice said, "and then whispered into my spiritual ear, 'Wow, this is SO cool, isn't it!'"

A Few Ruminations

A lot of ideas have floated around in my head over the last two years and a few of them have hit paper at one time or another. Sheri and I both learned a lot about life and death, both of which are natural events we will all experience.

ONE: Bad Events

Your attention is focused in one direction, like it is in all facets of life. It's a direction you did not choose but one you must follow because the Universe has chosen it for you. What you do with it is your business. You can become bitter or enlightened. You can become sad or hopeful. The event is an event. Only your reaction to it matters and your reaction tells volumes about who you are. No matter what, live a full life.

The experience will bring you both closer together as a couple as you face this challenge together. Whatever the result, you will live the life you have to the fullest possible level.

The process is over. The journey begins. Sheri lives in her new world and I live with her completed journey.

TWO: Living in the Now

Most people think we have all the time in the world to rectify the wrongs of our past, until we are brought up short by the appearance of an ugly, fatal disease.

Answer: Live our lives as if the next day might be our last. Get right with the world while you still have the opportunity because when it is too late, it is too late forever.

When you live as if the next day may be your last, you live in the moment and celebrate the life you have. It does not matter how or when we go. What matters is how we use the time we have. Mozart died in his thirties but left us sublime music from the years he had. Others live 90 years and leave little behind. We enjoy our days because they are the only ones we have. When our days are over, we leave content with the knowledge we lived well and made a difference when we could. Nothing else matters.

THREE: The Value of Time

For most of our lives, we exist, we work here, play there, and let the great stream of time sail by as if we had an infinite amount of it. A new day will always come.

When you get the sudden wake-up call of a fatal illness, it focuses your attitude. For us, this focus took a while. We didn't know the diagnosis for six months. When it came, we knew we might not get our next 20 years together. Then the ones we still had become even more important.

Quality of life also became ever more important. We planned where we would go and what we might do for our spirits. When a deadline shows up, life takes on new meaning. In April, we shared a beautiful four days in Idyllwild, California where we read, wrote, thought and lived together. Away from the rush of the world, we saw the truth of life. It is beautiful and fragile; worth all the investment we make in it. We have only this moment and must make the best of it and all the others to come.

FOUR: The Power of Forgiveness

What happens in the shadow world between life and death? This book tells the story of how one woman, guided by her friends and husband, faced and resolved her fears while she hovered unconscious on the edge of death.

This book is a wake-up call to resolve old grievances and grudges, forgive yourself and ask forgiveness of everyone you have hurt in your life and forgive others who have hurt you before you begin your journey to the next world.

Forgiveness is God's gift to mankind. We don't earn it, we accept it. When we forgive, we gain a lost life back.

FIVE: React to Reality, Not Expectations

When you don't know what's wrong, you imagine all kinds of possibilities, most of them bad. People do this all the time. We see a situation and extrapolate the worst from it. The worst seldom happens. It is better to let the situation develop as it is. Worrying does not make a difference. In most cases the result is between the worst and best.

When you get an answer, you can start to plan. However, do not go to the first perceived result. Live it day by day in the most positive attitude possible and see the value in whatever happens, no matter how dire. React to the events, not the speculations, which exist only in our imaginations.

SIX: The Future Will Plan Itself for You

The future is like a prairie that extends into the distance. The area closest to you is clear but as you look farther, the future blurs into unknowability. Its flat surface may be filled with hidden potholes and dangerous plants as well as tasty fruits and vegetables.

To plan your trek into the future is to navigate a minefield. Insurance is a given but what kind? How do you know which pothole you will fall into or which fruit you will encounter? You don't. When you buy insurance, you make a bet you will hit one pothole and not another. You guess, you buy, and you see what happens. The odds against success are great. We played two Royal Flushes in a row. Can't tell you how but what a difference it made.

I never planned my most successful decisions. The best choices emerged from the intuition of the moment. Listen to your inner sense and you cannot go wrong.

SEVEN: The Power of Together

When you pay attention to your wife or husband, you strengthen the relationship and become much closer. We did more together, we came to trust each other more and more and shared our feelings in more depth. I understood her needs more than ever and realize life can change or end at any time. We valued our time together like never before. No matter how long we have together, we live better and give each other a better life. In the end, we will have shared more and better than ever.

I remember one day, about October or so, when we talked about the mess so far.

She said, "I don't know if I would be alive today if not for your presence and caring."

This is why it is important to work together. In many ways, we both had the illness. She experienced it. I experienced her with it. When she couldn't cope, I coped for her and showed her what I experienced with my actions. In her moments of despair, I talked her through it, no matter the inconvenience.

Later, when I brought our dog to our evenings in rehab, she expressed such gratitude because little Sally meant so much to her. When I took care of the medications, she was grateful because she could not yet cope. It is important to stand up and do what is right. Nobody wants to hurt you or her. No blame exists, only support. We walked through every challenge together to the last day and it will always be thus.

www.ingramcontent.com/pod-product-compliance
Lightning Source LLC
Chambersburg PA
CBHW051817090426
42736CB00011B/1521